D0854986

The Jaguar E-type

The Jaguar E-type

A collector's guide
by Paul Skilleter

MOTOR RACING PUBLICATIONS LTD
28 Devonshire Road, Chiswick, London W4 2HD, England

First published 1979
Reprinted 1980
Reprinted 1981

ISBN 0 900549 46 7

Copyright © 1979 — Paul Skilleter and Motor Racing Publications Ltd

All rights reserved. No part of this publication may be reproduced,
stored in a retrieval system, or transmitted, in any form or by any
means, electronic, mechanical, photocopying, recording or otherwise,
without the prior permission of Motor Racing Publications Ltd

Photosetting by Zee Creative Ltd., London SE19
Printed in Great Britain by The Garden City Press Ltd.,
Letchworth, Hertfordshire

Contents

Introduction			7
Chapter 1	Ancestors and parentage	Mk VII, XKs and D-type	9
Chapter 2	Three Point Eight	1961 to 1964	17
Chapter 3	Four Point Two	1964 to 1971	37
Chapter 4	The E-type in competition	International to club events	57
Chapter 5	The Lightweight E-type	Jaguar's dashing dozen	73
Chapter 6	Five Point Three	1971 to 1975	83
Chapter 7	Buying an E-type	The choice, the examination and the test	101
Chapter 8	Spares and maintenance	Sources, manuals and clubs	109
Appendix A	Technical specifications		118
Appendix B	Chassis number sequences — by model and date		119
Appendix C	Engineering changes — by model, date and number		120
Appendix D	How fast? How economical? How heavy? — Performance figures		127
Appendix E	Production figures		128

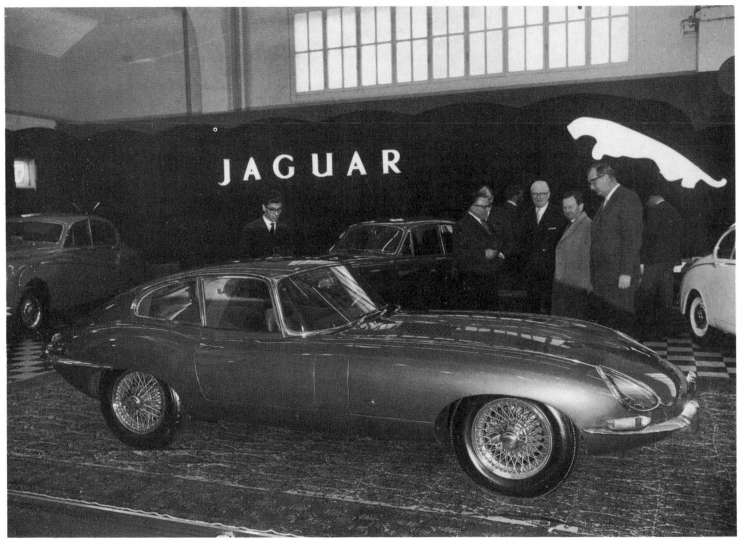

How it began — at the Geneva motor show, in March 1961. With Mk IX and Mk 2 saloons in the background, the new sports car formed the centrepiece of Jaguar's stand. Sir William Lyons (with pocket handkerchief) chats to journalists behind the car, together with William Heynes (left of group), who had been in overall charge of the E-type's engineering.

Introduction

The E-type Jaguar combines the assets of high performance and superb styling with a degree of practicality and reliability often far in advance of its very few contemporaries which are able to offer similar levels of performance motoring. So while an increasing number of E-types have been retired to a weekend or collector's-car status, sufficient are still being actively used to justify a good proportion of this book being devoted to the practical aspects of E-type ownership as distinct from the historical side.

Overall, I have tried to relate the E-type story concisely, and with the emphasis on facts. I have described the major differences between the models, how they evolved and what to look for when buying one of them. The essentials of E-type maintenance and restoration are also included, and the car's competition career is also outlined, with one chapter being devoted to the very special 'lightweight' E-type.

The Appendices to this book contain more data on the E-type than has been published previously, and will, I hope, be of considerable interest to enthusiasts and historians alike — though research of this type can never be truly complete.

In preparing this book, I would like to acknowledge the help given to me by Andrew Whyte of Jaguar Cars, Richard Foster of the JRT Press Office, and 3.8 and 5.3 owners Ray Dickens and Alan Hames, all of whom added much vital detail to the story.

If the E-type Jaguar is a car largely new to you, I hope I have provided you with an accurate portrait of it. If — like me — you are already an owner, I trust this book will help you to obtain even more from a truly remarkable motor car.

PAUL SKILLETER

January 1979

There have been only two distinct types of Jaguar sports car since the war, the E-type and the XK series which preceded it. First came the XK 120 in October 1948, essentially a short-chassis version of the MK VII to come, and a mobile test-bed for its new engine — the superbly successful twin-ohc XK engine, then of 3,442cc. It carried distinctive two-seater coachwork, originally of aluminium and ash-frame construction, before demand forced a change to pressed-steel. HKV 455, seen here with Prince Bira at Silverstone at the car's racing debut in 1949, was the very first XK 120 of all.

CHAPTER 1

Ancestors and parentage

Mk VII, XKs and D-type

The E-type Jaguar has its genesis in two cars — the Mk VII saloon of 1950 and the sports-racing D-type of 1954. During the war years, William Lyons — as he then was — had set himself the goal of producing a luxury 100-mph saloon as Jaguar's first all-new peacetime venture, and it was principally for the Mk VII that the superb twin-overhead-camshaft XK engine, ultimately to be used in the E-type, was designed and built. Then it was the Le Mans-winning D-type, with its advanced semi-monocoque construction, that provided all the main features of the E-type's body and chassis engineering.

But, of course, the E-type also came from a highly distinguished lineage of sports cars, going back to the beautifully proportioned, but strictly orthodox, SS 90 and SS 100 of 1935/36. Lyons' first sports car, the side-valve '90', had its origins in the controversial SS 1 of 1931, as it used a shortened version of its chassis frame; this, in fact, was carried over to the SS 100 of 1936, which although outwardly similar, possessed a number of refinements, including a Weslake-designed overhead-valve cylinder-head. Part of a new range of cars from SS, the '100' introduced the name 'Jaguar' to the motoring world.

The SS 100 acquitted itself well as a rapid (100 mph in 3½-litre form) and likeable sports car, besides recording some fine wins in international rallying, but coming at a time when the parent company's engineering department was only a few months old it added little to the progress of sports-car design. However, with the XK 120 of 1948, everything changed.

This sports car was as revolutionary then as the E-type was to be in 1961. The brilliantly engineered six-cylinder power unit could smoothly push it to a genuine 120 mph maximum, while its sophisticated, torsion-bar independent front suspension — also designed primarily for the Mk VII, but used meanwhile on the stop-gap Mk V saloon — gave a standard of ride comfort that was the best of any sports car then in production. In short, the XK 120 Jaguar was quicker, smoother and easier to drive and maintain than any other high-performance car in the world, and somehow, Lyons had contrived to make it cheaper, as well; at £998 basic, the XK 120 undersold its few potential rivals by hundreds, if not thousands, of pounds.

So instead of being a mere try-out for the Mk VII engine, the XK 120 became a full-scale commercial success in its own right, with enough orders taken at the October 1948 Motor Show in London to justify the factory laying down a proper production line, instead of just assembling a few cars a week by hand as had originally been the intention. From then on, right up to the demise of the E-type itself, Jaguar always catalogued a two-seater sports car.

The basic concept of the XK 120 continued to serve for another 13 years, although the original chassis was updated at intervals to become the XK 140 of 1954, and the XK 150 of 1957. The XK 140 retained the same body styling, but was given rack-and-pinion steering and tougher bumpers, while the XK 150 had updated lines and the big advantage of disc brakes — earlier XKs had been rather too fast for their overworked drums. All three variants established an important niche in overseas markets, particularly North America, where soon the E-type was to do so well.

Meanwhile, to push sales in these markets, Jaguar had embarked on a competition programme. By and large, this was

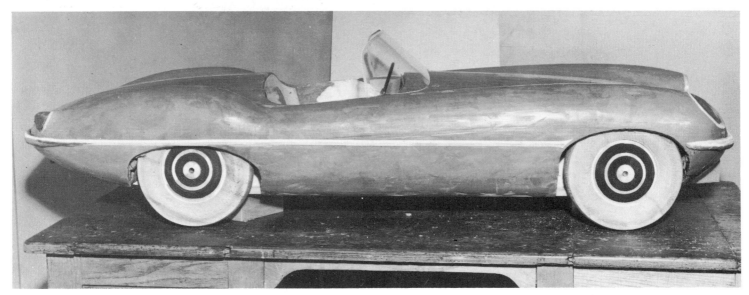

This 1954 Plasticine model is the earliest indication of the direction in which Jaguar were thinking in connection with a road sports car based on the D-type's shape. Although it corresponds more closely to the rare XKSS, of which 16 were produced in 1957 and which was simply a D-type with road equipment, all the main ingredients of the E-type can be seen. The model was almost certainly made by Malcolm Sayer.

limited to the Le Mans 24-hours race because that brought the most publicity. The new car built for the 1951 event won outright, and with more power and disc brakes this simple but effective tubular-framed car — the C-type — was victorious again in 1953.

The worldwide acclaim which these wins brought astonished even Jaguar, and to continue their campaign in 1954 an entirely new car was constructed — the D-type Jaguar. This superb machine was to become a classic in its own time, and remains today one of the best-known and most respected sports-racing cars in existence. While minor problems prevented a win in 1954, the D-type achieved its goal in 1955 and 1956, while in the 1957 race it totally devastated the Ferrari and Maserati opposition by finishing in 1st, 2nd, 3rd, 4th and 6th places.

While it was built strictly for racing, the D-type Jaguar nevertheless pointed very strongly towards the E-type in all its basic essentials. Taking shape under the watchful eye of William Heynes, Jaguar's chief engineer since 1935, the car displayed some very advanced features. It had a monocoque centre-section made up of two big hollow sills joined at either end by bulkheads, all made of aluminium and riveted together, aircraft fashion. Carrying the engine and front suspension was a triangulated framework which anchored on to the front bulkhead — although four of the major frame members also went through the bulkhead either side of the gearbox to meet the boxed rear bulkhead. In later D-types, the entire framework could be unbolted and withdrawn from the alloy centre-section in one piece instead of being welded in position, which made both repair and maintenance much easier.

The car was powered by a developed version of the original XK 120 engine, with the added sophistication of dry-sump lubrication and Weber carburettors. Front suspension was also similar to that of the XK 120, with double wishbones and torsion bars. The rear suspension was cantilevered from the rear bulkhead by four trailing-arms, and sprung by a torsion bar mounted crosswise along the bottom of the bulkhead.

But it was also in looks that the D-type foreshadowed the E-type. The shape of the car was in the gifted hands of the late Malcolm Sayer, who used very different methods, both from Sir William — who liked working with full-scale 'mock-ups' — and from most other motor body designers of the time, who generally began with styling sketches.

Sayer's ultimate aim was to produce a shape which needed the least amount of horsepower to push it through the air, and his approach to the task was probably unique in the motor industry at that time. He would start with the four basic dimensions which were dictated by the engineering requirements — length, width, height and ground clearance. Then, to arrive at the basic outline of the body around these fixed dimensions, he would use the simple mathematical formula for an ellipse to produce his lines on the drawing-board. Having achieved the car's side, plan and head-on views, Sayer would continue to use the ellipse formula to determine the shape of the entire skin surface of the car at all points, backed-up by wind-tunnel tests using one-tenth-scale models.

This very mathematical expression of shape hardly does justice to the real beauty of the contours which emerged on the finished car; no matter that the D-type Jaguar was about the most aerodynamically efficient racing car of its time, it was — and has remained — one of the most graceful and elegant sports cars ever built, too. That the E-type when it arrived possessed the D-type's major engineering *and* styling features goes a long way towards explaining its overwhelming success.

Before we come to the first true E-type prototype, it is worth taking a look at the D-type's intended successor, an experimental sports-racing car codenamed E2A, which foreshadowed some technical aspects of the E-type. E2A was built in the late-fifties, after Jaguar had officially retired from racing in 1956 (the 1957 victory had been gained by the private team of *Ecurie Ecosse)*, and it would have formed part of an official works team for Le Mans had Jaguar decided to return to racing.

Its all-alloy construction was similar to the D-type's, with a central tub and a detachable front subframe carrying the engine. The bonnet, like the D-type's, was non-stressed, but unlike that

The last of the XKs, the XK 150, had only been announced a few months when the first E-type prototype was conceived at Browns Lane. E1A, as it was termed, was under construction before the end of 1957, and was running by spring 1958. Very D-type in appearance, it had similar light-alloy body construction, with a front tubular subframe attached to a central monocoque — though unlike on the eventual E-type, these were not detachable. Smaller than the E-type, the prototype was powered by a 2.4-litre XK engine, and served to evaluate suspension and general chassis design. No hood was fitted, and only the bare legal requirements in the way of lighting — just sidelights. Wrap-round sidescreens were provided, though. Soon after the E-type proper entered production, E1A was broken up at the factory.

Cockpit view of E1A, showing the aircraft-type riveting of the alloy panels and the generally functional build. Note that E1A was given footwells, which were absent from the first few E-types, also the lack of that familiar bulge in the bonnet. A sidelight can be seen far right, and a dash-mounted stopwatch on the extreme left.

The top of the conventional Salisbury final-drive unit of this car was anchored to a deep, transverse box-member in the rear of the monocoque section, and braced by diagonal supports running from the rear bulkhead. The disc brakes were inboard, adjacent to the differential housing, and running from them to the wheels were fixed-length drive-shafts with double universal joints, which also formed the upper arms of the wishbone system. The main loads, though, were taken by the lower wishbones, of strong, fabricated box-construction with wide-based inner mountings on a subframe fixed underneath the final-drive casing. The outer ends of the wishbones were pivotted on to a big aluminium upright on each side, which contained two taper-roller bearings for the wheel hubs. Combined coil spring/damper units, two on each side, were anchored to the lower wishbones via transverse taper pins. An anti-roll bar was fitted, and the only essential differences between this suspension and the E-type's were the lack of trailing radius-arms, and the absence of a steel 'cradle' containing the suspension as a unit.

The car's appearance at Le Mans was ill-fated; painted in Cunningham's American racing colours the white-and-blue car may have 'upheld Jaguar's reputation for being beautifully prepared', as one scribe noted, but was in trouble from the second lap onwards. It was a breakage of the fuel-injection pipe to the pump which probably accounted for the car's final demise at 1.40 am on the Sunday, because although the fracture was repaired, the engine was apparently running on a very weak mixture thereafter, which may have been the indirect cause of the head-gasket failure which eventually sidelined the car for good.

Afterwards, Briggs Cunningham took E2A home with him, complete with a 3.8-litre engine this time, as opposed to the 3-litre unit which met the decreed maximum capacity for Le Mans after 1957. But only sporadic success attended the car's racing appearances in North America, and it was soon retired from active service, later returning to Great Britain, where it is now a unique exhibit in Guy Griffiths' collection of Jaguars at Chipping Campden, in Gloucestershire.

But while it may have had some features in common with the E-type, E2A was strictly a competition project and was in no way an E-type prototype as such. By the time E2A went to Le Mans (probably against the factory's better judgment, but how do you refuse one of your most important USA distributors and

on the previous car the bodywork aft of the rear bulkhead behind the driver was stressed and couldn't be removed. The full-width windscreen and high tail were features required by the regulations of the period.

But of the greatest interest to those who saw the car emerge for the first time in public at the Le Mans test days of 1960 — in the hands of private entrant Briggs Cunningham, to whom it had been lent — was the rear suspension. For the first time Jaguar had 'gone independent' at the rear, and the system featured many of the ideas which were to appear on the E-type less than a year later.

America's greatest Jaguar enthusiast?) the production E-type was already running, and the first prototype was getting on for three years old.

This latter car was a fascinating little device. They called it E1A at Browns Lane, the 'A' standing for aluminium, the material which was used for its construction — light alloy being easier to manipulate for one-off projects. It had been Jaguar's war work which had led them to the use of alloy for their racing cars and prototypes, their fitters having gained much useful expertise in the use of this material during the repair or manufacture of parts for such aircraft as Whitley and Wellington bombers — plus the aircraft background of such key men as Malcolm Sayer.

E1A was built to test and prove the major design features which were intended for the next Jaguar sports car, the successor to the XK 150, and it paralleled other experiments with independent rear suspension which was also to be adopted for the unitary-construction Mk 10 Jaguar saloon, the replacement for the Mk IX derivative of the Mk VII. The Mk IX, like the XK 150 whose chassis and running gear it shared, was getting distinctly long in the tooth, and like the XK it was in danger of being left behind by continental rivals such as the Mercedes-Benz — especially on ride comfort and handling.

Rather smaller than the E-type to come, E1A nevertheless had the same basic appearance — a 'smoothed-out' version of the D-type's shape. It was shorter than the 'E', and of narrower track and lower build; construction was on D-type principles, with a centre monocoque-section fashioned out of aluminium with aircraft riveting. Two big hollow sills and a 'horseshoe' front bulkhead provided most of the strength. Like the original 1954 D-types, the triangulated frame carrying the engine and front suspension was in magnesium alloy and was not detachable from the centre-section. This frame allowed a non-stressed nose/bonnet section to be used, which hinged forward on pivots at the front, but the strictly utilitarian aspect of the little car was underlined

The E-type's shape was a re-interpretation of the D-type Jaguar's, as this photograph of the two cars clearly shows. The sports-racer's lines were softened and slightly elongated, but virtually all the major features were mirrored in the new road car. The two cars shared the same track, but at 8 ft the E-type's wheelbase was the greater by about 6 inches; mechanical similarities were marked, too, although the D-type had a 'solid' rear axle sprung by a transverse torsion-bar, instead of the E-type's sophisticated new independent rear suspension. These cars were photographed during the 1964 six-hours race at Silverstone, and were part of the Jaguar Drivers Club team.

13

Making its first public appearance almost a year before the E-type's launch, E2A raced at Le Mans in 1960 with a 3-litre D-type engine, entered by Briggs Cunningham; it failed to finish, but it provided an advance view of Jaguar's new independent rear suspension, and it hinted even more strongly than the D-type of the still-secret road car's looks. E2A itself was an intended successor to the D-type and was purely a racing prototype — by 1960 the first E-type had already been built.

by the absence of headlights — just sidelights at the base of the wraparound screen to satisfy the requirements of the law. The interior of the car was bereft of trim, just seats for the driver and passenger, who were surrounded by areas of unpainted aluminium and hundreds of rivet heads. A wood-rimmed steering wheel and black-painted facia with central instruments faced the driver.

The car was powered by a 2.4-litre engine borrowed from the Mk 1 saloon, the drive being transmitted by a Jaguar gearbox to the rear end, which featured the E-type's rear suspension in embryo form. At first, twin swinging links were used here to carry the wheel hubs, but later the method of using a fixed-length (non-splined) half-shaft to do the job of the top link was evolved.

At this stage, the differential was bolted directly to steel reinforced parts of the monocoque, but it soon became clear that noise and vibration would make this arrangement very undesirable for a road car, which is why the E-type was to be given its steel bridge-member to house the entire rear-suspension set-up. This enabled the whole package to be insulated from the monocoque, and made servicing easier because the assembly could be dropped as a complete unit from the car.

Construction of E1A began towards the end of 1957 and was completed by the spring of 1958. The car was to have a hard and busy life, both at the Motor Industry Research Association's test ground at Lindley, near Nuneaton, and while undergoing extensive trials on the road, often journeying to Wales, a convenient run from Coventry, which included all types of road with relatively little traffic to get in the way.

Such test runs were usually carried out by the development staff, including Norman Dewis, Phil Weaver (who remembers that the low build of the car often resulted in a cracked sump if drivers were over-exuberant) and Bill Heynes himself. But one person outside the factory who was allowed the privilege of driving E1A was Christopher Jennings, then editor of *The Motor*.

Chris Jennings was one of the few people outside Browns Lane who enjoyed a really close relationship with the factory — or indeed with Lyons himself. This association went back many years, for Mr. Jennings' wife Margaret, as Miss Allen, had driven in the SS1 works team before the war. Knowing that Jennings had a favourite test route consisting of 48½ miles of Welsh roads between St Peter's Church, Carmarthen, and the River Bridge at

Brecon, Lyons invited him and his wife to try this 'entirely new model' and compare it with other fast cars they'd driven across the same route — particularly the Aston Martin with Le Mans engine and disc brakes which had been the quickest over the route so far.

'The result was almost fantastic', wrote Jennings later, having averaged a startling 67.7 mph over that undulating route, some seven minutes quicker than the Aston. 'It will be seen, therefore', he went on, 'that the new Jaguar is a potential world-beater . . .' which turned out to be a very accurate prediction. Jennings also remarked that he envisaged a road-test maximum speed for the production car of 'not very far short of 150 mph, which is going to make us think'; it made Jaguar think, too, with repercussions which will be revealed later!

By the time that Jennings borrowed E1A for that memorable run — in May 1958 — the true production prototype for the E-type had also been completed. This car had rather a strange birth; it was originally assembled by pop-riveting formed steel sheets together to make what was really only a non-running mock-

Jaguar's experimentation with independent rear suspension dated back at least to 1944, when two 'baby Jeeps' had been completed; one was powered by a 1,096cc JAP engine, but the VB prototype shown here had a Ford 10 engine. More interestingly, the power was transmitted via a solidly mounted differential and two half-shafts, which ran to big hub-carriers suspended by coil springs — very much E-type practice. The project was not proceeded with as the new generation of transport aircraft were able to carry a full-weight Jeep.

The 3,781cc engine in the E-type had already been in service since October 1959, when it had appeared in the XK 150. The 3.8 unit was developed from the 3.4 in order to give more torque, mainly for the saloon cars, and the Mk IX saloon was also given the new engine. A new head was also developed, and was an option on the XK 150 together with triple 2-inch SU carburettors, when the car was known as the XK 150S. The 3.8 'S' engine, as can be seen here installed in an open two-seater XK 150, was used virtually unchanged in the E-type.

15

This was the first full-size E-type prototype, photographed at the factory in 1959. The body shape has been finalized, but detail design has not — note the lack of front sidelights, and the temporary use of what seem to be 'Mk 1' Jaguar saloon rear lights, turned on their sides. The bonnet is fastened using an exterior handle, like the C-type Jaguar, but unlike the early production cars with their 'T' handles, and later cars with the internal bonnet locks.

up, from which dimensions could be taken and to which various items of equipment could be offered up. 'Then,' recalls Phil Weaver, 'one day Heynes rang up Experimental and asked if they could get the shell running!' So it was a case of setting-to and replacing the rivets with spot-welds and braze, to create the first full-size E-type prototype. But while it covered many thousands of miles on the test fleet, to sort out the many hundreds of detail points which have to be finalized on a production car, it never lost its nickname of the 'Pop Rivet Special'.

Besides these two prototypes, further development work was also carried out using a Mk 2 saloon, into which was fitted the production-type independent rear suspension, and this, too, covered many tens of thousands of test miles. The eventual fate of the prototypes? Their work done, they were cut into four pieces and thrown on the scrap-heap — the launch of the 'real' E-type was imminent, and Jaguar had more important things to worry about than potential museum pieces.

CHAPTER 2

Three Point Eight

1961 to 1964

Nineteen sixty-one was an optimistic year. In Britain, the final restraints imposed by an austere economic policy in the early postwar years were at last forgotten, and the motor industry was almost buoyant. For the sports-car driver, if he had but realised it, the 'swinging sixties' were to represent the golden years of the British open sports car, before the traditional concept of uncluttered lines and free-breathing engines was to be virtually destroyed by Ralph Nader and the US Federal Government.

The sixties added science to the art of building a sports car, so that you had cars which not just looked good, but also handled and stopped efficiently, departments in which their illustrious forebears were sometimes found to be lacking; the better sports cars of the fifties might have handled quite well, but they often had a heavy, stubborn feel about them. The E-type, despite its size, felt light and responsive; and this, together with an efficient engine and a brilliant clarity of line, makes it a car which some might call the climax of the true British sports car.

The big international motor show at Geneva in Switzerland was chosen for the E-type's launch in March 1961, and the impact it made was enormous. 'Nothing else which is on view can challenge Sir William Lyons' new model for the "car of the show" title' wrote Joe Lowrey for *The Motor,* and the new model received immediate acclaim from the world's motoring press.

That the car on Jaguar's show stand was a fixed-head coupe is a case for mild surprise because, as we have seen, the open-two-seater model was envisaged originally — the sleek coupe came much later in the design programme. Two cars went to Geneva, one for display and one for demonstration purposes. On the stand was (almost certainly) commission number 885005, the fifth left-hand-drive fixed-head built; after the show it was sold to a Geneva dealer and is now lost, but its sister car, 885002, registered 9600 HP and driven out to Geneva by Bob Berry of Jaguar's publication relations staff as the press demonstrator, survives to this day after a hectic early life in the hands of the British motoring press and a dozen tough road tests.

The production E-type was a remarkable piece of engineering, and is one of the most clear-cut examples of what were purely racing design features being transferred to a road car. The full circle had been turned — Jaguar's original competition car, the C-type, had been largely built from XK 120 components; now, Jaguar's latest road sports car had successfully embodied all the main ingredients of their greatest sports-racing car, the D-type.

This was evident from the first glance at the new machine — Malcolm Sayer had continued his mathematical ellipse formula from the D-type, softening a curve here, blending a line there and, with the aid of Sir William's own instinctive eye for form, discreetly incorporating all the necessary appendages of a practical road-going car to produce a final result which has been hailed as one of the greatest automotive designs of all time — a near-perfect blend of mathematics and pure art, no less.

Just as with the D-type, the E-type was made up of two halves. The major part of the car was its stressed-skin centre and rear section, which formed the passenger compartment and carried the rear-suspension assembly. It was built up from a number of mainly 20-gauge steel panels, the main outer panels having been made on stretcher presses, and the smaller ones on rubber die presses — virtually all by outside suppliers such as Pressed Steel Fisher.

The 'show' launch of the E-type at Geneva was quite dramatic, the car being unveiled in front of the assembled press and VIPs by hoisting up a huge box which concealed it. As can be seen there was spontaneous applause, and no wonder — Jaguar had scooped the occasion. The fixed-head on display (no.5, left-hand drive) showed some of the features displayed by very early E-types, including the mounting of the reversing light adjacent to the left-hand overrider — this was soon repositioned above the exhaust pipes.

These panels were welded together on jigs, which meant Jaguar employing some new techniques, including the use of carbon dioxide wire-welding plant. The main structural members of the assembly were the two big hollow sills running the length of the monocoque. At their front end two vertical box-sections rose to form the bulkhead and scuttle, with dog-leg hollow extensions projecting backwards on each side at the top to take the windscreen side pillars. The steel floor ran from the inner member of each sill to the transmission tunnel in the middle, which thus became a stressed member, the floor also being strengthened by a transverse box-member which ran under the seats. Behind the seats was a low rear bulkhead joining the sills and providing the major structural support for the rear-end of the car. Arched box-members ran from the rear bulkhead to hold the rear-suspension cradle, and were welded to the inner wheelarches and the boot floor. The outer rear wing pressings, and the roof on the fixed-head, all contributed to stiffness as well.

Additionally, the rear bulkhead was braced internally by five 'boxes' on either side of the transmission tunnel, partly because it was also the mounting point for the rear suspension's two trailing-arms. Inside the sills, 10-inch wide flitch plates ran diagonally from outer top to inner bottom at the four points where the front and rear bulkheads met the sills.

All this may seem a bit complicated, but it is essential to grasp if you want to know how an E-type was built-up, and thus to understand why it rusts and how to repair it, which we will touch on in another chapter. Studying the pictures elsewhere in this book will help, too. But corrosion apart, the monocoque was strong enough, although by modern standards the torsional stiffness of the open cars was not particularly brilliant.

Bolting on to the front bulkhead, via eight attachment points, was the detachable framework holding the engine and front suspension, made up from Reynolds 5H square-section tubing with additional tubular bracing. This frame could be further dismantled into three separate pieces — the two side-members and the square front cross-member. Outrigged from this front member was a further detachable frame which held the radiator and the bonnet pivots.

That beautiful, long-snouted steel bonnet could be detached as a unit, and be further disassembled. Besides the internal splash guards, it was made up of three main parts — the big centre-section containing those characteristic louvres, and the two outer wings. The lower part of the nose was also a separate component and could be unbolted. The bonnet hinged forward, of course, and was counterbalanced by coil springs; compared with the previous XK models, access to the engine was delightfully easy.

We have not said much about the E-type's power plant, but most people will be familiar with Jaguar's famous six-cylinder engine which created that initial furore in the 120mph XK 120 of 1948; it still powers most of the Jaguar saloons made today, in one form or another, despite the big flat-head V12 which appeared in the early-seventies. For Jaguar, the engine gave the least aggravation of all in the development of the E-type, because the triple-carburettor, 3,781cc 'S' version of the XK engine, which had been an option in the later XK 150s, provided ample power and could be dropped straight into the new car with virtually no modification.

The 87 x 106 mm engine had been developed from the original 83 x 106 mm, 3,442cc unit of the XK 120 and Mk VII, mainly to provide more torque (up from 216 lb ft to 240 lb ft) and thus better top-gear acceleration for the Mk IX saloon. It was offered in the XK 150, at first with the standard 'B-type' cylinder-head, then later with the 'straight-port' version, which had similar valve sizes and camshafts, but better gas-flow. Three instead of two SU carburettors were fitted, of larger (2-inch) choke diameter, and despite a portly 29cwt, the last and the fastest of the XKs could certainly motor — to 60mph in 7.6 seconds, and to 100mph in 19 seconds, with a top speed of 136mph.

Long before it was mated with the E-type to provide one of the most successful partnerships ever, the XK engine had acquired a legendary reputation for strength and long life. The tough, seven-

The construction of the E-type was unique amongst road cars, and was taken directly from the sports-racing D-type. The triangulated front subframe was secured to the monocoque by eight bolt-on attachment points, and could itself be unbolted into three separate units. The lower members adjacent to the transmission tunnel also carried the front suspension torsion-bar anchorages.

bearing crankshaft could take anything handed out to it, while power and efficiency was ensured by the advanced, all-aluminium cylinder-head with its classic configuration of twin overhead camshafts and Weslake hemispherical combustion chambers. As installed in the E-type it was rated at 265 bhp by Jaguar; this was certainly rather optimistic, the figure being in retaliation to the North American horsepower race; in practice, you'd have been fortunate to see a genuine 220 bhp at the flywheel of an installed

Extending forward from the main frame was a lighter subframe which held the radiator and bonnet hinges. Much of the body stiffness was provided by the big outer sills, the horseshoe-shaped front bulkhead and the low rear bulkhead which ran between the rear-wheel arches. The roof and upper rear quarters were all stressed as well on the fixed-head.

unit, but that is by-the-way — the E-type performed very well, whatever were the 'paper' figures.

The engine was mated to a gearbox which, of all the E-type's equipment, attracted the most criticism from press and owners alike. This old-fashioned relic from XK days and beyond (Henry Manney III alleged it had been designed by Levassor) had no synchromesh on first gear and very little on the others. Its one virtue was that it rarely broke, and its life was usually measured in decades rather than miles. But the modernity of the E-type's design showed up its failings all too well, even though Jaguar took over production of the box from Moss in order to improve quality. Jaguar diehards claimed that there was much satisfaction in the concentration necessary to achieve a clean change, but this did not impress the average North American promenader accustomed to MG flick-switches or two-pedal Hydramatics.

Between the engine and the gearbox was a 10-inch Borg & Beck single-plate clutch; this was hydraulically operated, and indeed some complaints of the gearbox being stiff can be traced back to a leaking clutch master or slave cylinder preventing complete disengagement. The clutch, too, was generally long-lasting, with an average life of at least 30,000 miles, though much more has

been known — my own 1962 fixed-head, for example, showed no signs of the necessary engine removal for a new clutch (and hasn't suffered the hatchet-job on the transmission tunnel that is the only other alternative) after at least 100,000 miles, 40,000 of them mine, and this is by no means a record.

Sharing the forward subframe with the engine was the front suspension, a double-wishbone, torsion-bar system almost identical to that of the D-type, which in turn was a modified edition of Jaguar's first independent front suspension developed by William Heynes for the Mk V, Mk VII and XK 120. It used slender forged wishbones top and bottom, with upper and lower ball pivots; springing was by torsion bar, which anchored to the bottom wishbone via an inboard extension of the arm — this had the effect of bending the bar, besides twisting it, and made it possible to remove the torsion bar without having to dismantle most of the suspension, which you had to do on an XK. The bar's rearward anchorage was under the scuttle, where vernier spline adjustment was possible; the ride rate per wheel was 100 lb in.

As well as being light and efficient, this suspension was very hardy, with long-lasting Metalastic wishbone inner mountings, and providing they were kept greased, the two ball-joints on either side could last well into the 100,000-mile figure. The front roll centre was 4½ inches, which was quite high, but roll was kept down by the use of an anti-roll bar connected to the outer ends of each lower wishbone. Telescopic shock absorbers provided the damping.

Much praise had been heaped upon the E-type's steering, which was both direct (2½ turns lock-to-lock) and, for a big car, very light; it did much towards giving the E-type that agile feel which was such a revelation in 1961. Jaguar had been using rack-and-pinion steering on their sports cars since the 1951 C-type, and that was the system used on the E-type. The rack ran behind the radiator and was connected to the steering wheel by a universally jointed steering column, which was adjustable. On earlier cars the upper and inner steering column housed two felt bearings which, if not kept oiled, could give rise to a mysterious slackness in the steering.

A word on that classic wood-rimmed wheel. It was made by the Coventry Timber Bending Co. Ltd., who had supplied Jaguar with their wood-rimmed steering wheels since the days of the D-types, and it was constructed from eight 3 mm beech veneers 5½ feet long and 4 inches wide. These were bonded together and cured by low-frequency heating, then sliced into four pieces, to make four wheels. Each wheel was then split again and recessed to take the drilled aluminium 'spider', bonded again, then hand-finished and polished on a lathe. A little piece of olde English craftsmanship all of its own.

But the *pièce de résistance* of the new car was probably its rear suspension — independence at the blunt end was still unusual in Great Britain, where cart springs and a rigid axle were still the norm, while the North American motor industry was just as, if not even more, conservative in this respect. The reasons were mainly cost and the technical difficulties of producing a system which kept the wheels at the right angles whatever the car was doing. Making the rear wheels independent could also take up more room, so most manufacturers were willing to accept lesser standards of ride, handling on rough surfaces, and tyre-to-road power transference in return for an easier life on the production side.

Not so Jaguar. Well aware that full independence would soon become standardized on higher-priced rivals, and sensitive to justifiable criticism from the motoring press of the tendency of

The E-type's bodyshell was made up of a number of pressed-steel panels which were spot-welded together on a jig, the exposed joins being filled and contoured by lead-loading. The whole structure was very rigid, especially on the fixed-head with its big roof panel. Inside, access holes to the rear brake pads can be seen; these are normally covered by a removable plate. The deep tail-section held the spare wheel and petrol tank.

This is almost certainly the first fixed-head coming together. Front bumpers are non-standard, lacking the indentation below the sidelights which have yet to be fitted, and so is the overrider. The grille bar carries a temporary 'XK 150' bonnet badge instead of the production E-type badge.

E-type fixed-head shell assembly in the experimental body shop, pre-production. The seam between body and sill has not yet been lead-filled; the seam at the rear is normally covered by the rear bumper. The object in the foreground is not a Jaguar V12, but just a stand for two cylinder-heads!

the XK 150 and Mk IX Jaguars towards axle tramp under hard acceleration and their inability to match comfort with such as Citroen's DS model, the engineering department knew that if they were not to be left behind in ride and handling qualities the rear wheels had to be separated. Jaguar's new Mk IX saloon replacement — the unitary construction Mk 10 — and the new sports car were both included in this resolve.

In production form, the suspension was much as described in connection with E1A, but with certain refinements. To eliminate noise, the differential, with its inboard discs, drive-shafts and tubular lower wishbones, was mounted inside a steel bridge piece, which was bolted into the car through four rubber-bonded mountings. The production E-type also had two additional suspension components — two radius-arms which ran forward from the lower wishbones to anchorage points under the car behind the seats. Here they were bolted in place via conical rubber/metal blocks so that throughout the system metal-to-metal contact between suspension and car was completely absent. This self-contained suspension unit could in fact be detached in one piece within as little as 15 minutes.

Big cast-aluminium carriers held the two opposed taper-roller hub bearings — the outer part of the hub was of course splined to take the 5-inch rim, 15-inch diameter wire wheels which were standard equipment (a 5½-inch wheel was available for rear fitment only as a racing extra, along with R5 racing tyres instead of the normal Dunlop RS5 road tyres). An anti-roll bar was fitted, while the lower links also took the two-pairs-per-side coil spring/damper units.

Inside the Salisbury hypoid final-drive unit was a Powr-Lok differential, which had also been standard on the XK 150S. This consisted in principle of multi-plate clutches adjacent to the differential side gears, which, on one road wheel finding less adhesion than the other, would be loaded by both springs and a system of cams to provide traction which would otherwise be 'leaked' through the spinning wheel. The Powr-Lok was not an integral part of this Salisbury differential and could be added to any similar unit, although it was standard on the E-type. It worked well, and combined with the carefully thought-out geometry of the E-type's suspension, gave the car outstanding traction, although with fierce driving the (replaceable) clutches could wear out relatively quickly.

Brakes on the 3.8 E-type are a slightly controversial subject. Basically, they were Dunlop disc brakes, similar in design to the equipment used on the much heavier (29 cwt) XK 150, having 11-inch discs front and 10-inch rear with two wheel-cylinders working on each. Their major peculiarity was Jaguar's use of an American brake servo, the Kelsey Hayes unit made in Britain under licence by Dunlop. A feature of this equipment was that it applied a mechanical pressure to the twin master cylinders (via a balance bar operated by the brake pedal) instead of the more normal 'line pressure' boost given by conventional servos as used on, for instance, the Mk IX and Mk 2 Jaguar saloons.

Possibly it was not quite man enough for the job, or the

The XK engine in possibly its best and most efficient guise — the triple carburettor, 3,781cc unit ready to go into an E-type. Capable of six-figure mileages without overhaul, the engine usually outlasted the car's bodyshell. While some American owners did not consider that its electrical ancillaries maintained the same degree of reliability, about the only major fault of the power unit itself was a tendency towards high oil consumption — 200 or 300 miles to the pint, perhaps — caused by the linered bores flexing, which allowed oil to by-pass the piston rings, and through valve-guide loss in the cylinder-head.

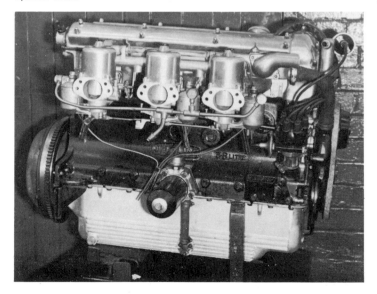

Exhaust-port aspect of the 3.8 XK engine. Oil consumption was later improved by a stiffer block, new piston rings and valve-guide seals. Exhaust manifolds were vitreous-enamelled, a generally long-lasting finish, although a sustained run at close to maximum speed would soon burn it off. The pipe at the rear of the block is the oil feed to the camshafts. The 11-pint sump was cast in aluminium.

remainder of the braking system just wasn't beefy enough to cope with the very high velocities that the E-type could attain at the drop of a hat. Certainly there were complaints of fade, and of delayed response to the pedal, and it is true that any serious competition work would cause them to wilt within two or three laps, as Graham Hill found when he drove the E-type in its first race. But — and this is probably the secret — if the 3.8's braking system was kept in top order, with the correct (hard) pads properly bedded in and fresh brake fluid, it was not as bad as its subsequent reputation appears to suggest. Owners of early cars with the original bellows servo still fitted (many were changed over to the later type used on the 4.2 E-type) should, before complaining too bitterly, ask themselves if they've ever taken the system completely apart and replaced every suspect item with the correct new part — remembering that we are talking about cars

Engine installation on the 3.8 E-type was carried out by lowering the frame/monocoque unit on to the engine and transmission, rather than by inserting the engine from above. This is a left-hand-drive car, with the heat-shielded brake and clutch fluid reservoirs located on the engine frame instead of on the bulkhead. Note the separate header tank, glass-fibre fan cowling and light-alloy radiator of the earlier cars. The heater fan and box are in the foreground, finished in black; the frame was painted in body colour, the front suspension in black or silver.

which are now 15 or more years old.

Twin master cylinders with independent fluid reservoirs provided a measure of 'fail safe' braking, though in the unlikely event of the front circuit failing, the inboard rear brakes alone were of little use; in any case, shrouded as they were by the rear suspension, the rear brakes were the first to overheat, mainly because the hot air could not get away. A concomitant problem was heat soak from brakes to differential, which despite its special heavy-duty seals could begin to leak oil. Gradual development finally eliminated this problem.

The handbrake on early cars was not self-adjusting, but after a few hundred roadsters and 19 fixed-heads were made, Jaguar introduced a self-adjusting ratchet mechanism for the device, which was cable-operated and had its own calipers. But buried out of sight, and out of mind, adjacent to the final-drive casing,

the enclosed ratchet was often neglected and consequently could seize up, making a not terribly efficient design almost useless.

Inside the E-type you sat very low behind your big wood-rimmed wheel, and in a true bucket seat. This was upholstered in non-quilted leather, with moquette on the rear of the squab, and was rather sparsely padded; also, there was a beading running across the squab which, if you happened to be the wrong shape, could quickly produce a calloused backbone on long runs. Furthermore, there was no rake adjustment, and on early cars not enough rearward movement of the seat, which meant that taller drivers found that the steering wheel could foul their thighs. Others complained of not enough headroom, so all in all the original E-type did not rate highly on creature comfort.

Efforts were made to improve things early on in production. By the end of 1961 the floor on each side of the console was given a well, which gave more legroom, and on the driver's side only, part of the rear bulkhead was cut away and a semi-circular indentation let in to give more rearward seat travel — the hasty nature of this last modification is underlined by the fact that in the fixed-head the new panel behind the seat was pop-riveted in place as initially there had not been time to incorporate the modification into the pressings making up this part of the rear-end, although this was done later.

Although the trim shop messed around with different sorts of padding in different places, the basic shape of the seats was not altered until the advent of the 4.2 E-type, when completely new seats were introduced. Speaking personally, as a 6-ft owner of an early 1962 fixed-head with floor wells and the better seat travel, I find the car quite comfortable and have no problems with headroom, but on the other hand I know of other owners who feel differently.

In front of the driver were two big round instruments,

The E-type's independent rear suspension, which is still in use today on the superb XJ saloon range. The differential unit can be seen bolted into the detachable subframe, with the drive-shafts running from it to the aluminium hub-carriers. The two pairs of coil spring/damper units act on the lower, tubular, suspension arms which pivot on wide-based mountings on the subframe. Further location is provided by the radius-arms, which mount to the car itself, via rubber Metalastic joints. This view of a very early E-type also shows the lack of footwells in the cockpit floor, which runs flat from front to rear.

Jaguar's classic hemispherical head, in E-type 'straight port' form. The siamesed inlet tracts from the SU carburettors are curved to provide equal lengths, while the head porting runs in a straight line from tract to inlet valve. Evolved by the late Harry Weslake, this made the XK engine even more efficient and it was difficult to achieve less than 18mpg with a 3.8 E-type whatever the conditions — in fact fairly gentle driving could result in 25mpg-plus.

indicating engine rpm and road speed in either mph or kph according to the market. Of classic Jaguar design, with crisp white lettering on a matt-black surface, these instruments represent one of the best detail features of all E-types. They were supported by a row of smaller dials in the centre of the facia monitoring amps, fuel, oil pressure and water temperature. The rather old-fashioned headlight switch was set in the middle, and below was a row of black flick switches controlling (from left to right on rhd cars) the interior light, panel light (two brightnesses), two-speed heater motor, console map light, windscreen washer and the two-speed, triple-blade wipers. Ignition was by key, and another antiquarian touch was provided by the separate starter button. The whole centre panel could be hinged down for attention after undoing a couple of knurled knobs.

On either side of the central instrument panel were slide controls for the heater and choke, respectively; unlike the XK 150, the latter was manually controlled. The not amazingly efficient heater, with its two-speed fan motor, used fresh air ducted from the nose (a similar duct on the other side of the

bonnet brought cool air to the big, drum-like air cleaner for the carburettors). Later, proper air conditioning was offered (at a cost of £100), but few 3.8 E-types seem to have had this extra fitted — possibly because it threw too much strain on the existing engine cooling system. In any case, only left-hand-drive cars could be so equipped because of the steering column position.

In fact the original E-type's cooling arrangements were rather marginal. Following D-type practice, a separate header tank was used, together with a radiator of light alloy (changed to copper during 1964). No engine-driven fan was fitted, but instead a rather overworked, windscreen-wiper-type electric motor propelled a single-blade cowled fan, which was controlled via a temperature sensor in the header tank. Provided you could keep moving, even if only at 20 or 30mph, enough air would flow through the nose to keep things cool, but heavy traffic on a hot day in (say) summertime New York could cause the temperature gauge to creep towards 100 degrees C with the fan on.

Even then, if the system was in good order it still wouldn't actually boil, but the margin was small. Several modifications were made by the factory before the completely revised, twin-fan system appeared on later 4.2 cars, such as a new header tank with internal modifications to provide a better flow, a 9-lb instead of a 4-lb radiator cap (which raised the boiling point), and a quick-lift thermostat. The sensor in the header tank was not particularly reliable, and failure of the fan to cut in when needed would

Another view of the E-type's rear suspension, showing how the bridge-type subframe bolts on to the car using rubber mounts. The calipers of the inboard rear discs can also be seen, as can the handbrake cables, although no automatic adjuster is fitted on this early example. Being on the experimental fleet, this car had a heat sensor fitted to the differential casing, as due to the inboard discs a critical temperature was sometimes reached, resulting in a partial failure of the output-shaft oil seals. The up-and-over anti-roll bar is visible top foreground.

This picture demonstrates how the independent rear end could be detached from the car as a complete unit, with trailing arms attached. Note the rubber mounting blocks, which are not dissimilar to engine mounts.

The E-type's front suspension was a twin-wishbone system sprung by torsion-bars and employing top and bottom outer ball-joints. The inner mountings of the wishbones were by Metalastic joints. The steering rack, the bellows of which can be seen, was also mounted to the subframe via a rubber/metal sandwich. The airbox on the left was made of glass-fibre, and led into a big steel air cleaner 'drum' which contained a renewable paper element; they were painted silver and black, respectively.

Jaguar, with Dunlop, pioneered the use of disc brakes on cars with the 1953 C-type; the XK 150 of 1957 had them as standard, so naturally this is how the E-type was stopped. One departure from previous practice was the brake booster, which incorporated a vacuum-motivated bellows which acted directly on the mechanical linkage to the master-cylinders (one each for front and rear). A vacuum reservoir tank was positioned underneath, accessible via a detachable panel. The independent brake-fluid reservoirs incorporated Sovy fluid-level warning lights. Running across the top of the bellows unit is part of the nicely engineered throttle linkage.

certainly lead to boiling — owners took to wiring the fan motor to earth via terminal W1 of the relay and a dashboard switch, so that the device could be operated manually and still retain the cut-in of the fan by the sensor as an overriding safety factor. But all this did little to improve cockpit temperatures, which could reach very uncomfortable levels due mainly to an insufficiently insulated transmission cover and to poor fresh-air ventilation.

Although marketed as a 'GT' model, luggage capacity for a truly Grand Tour was limited in the open two-seater E-type. The bootlid was opened by pulling a catch near the driver's seat, to disclose a rather shallow space with wooden floorboards covered by a Hardura mat. These could be removed for access to the spare wheel, and to the kidney-shaped fuel tank with its immersed Lucas fuel pump. The jack and tools were also stowed here in the spare-wheel well.

The fixed-head was somewhat better-off, the rear door giving access to quite a generous luggage platform which, on lowering a hinged panel, could extend right up to the seat backs. A useful number of suitcases could be stowed here, and if no passenger was being carried it was possible to use the entire length of the interior to absorb loads of a most unlikely length — objects over 7-ft long could be accommodated with the rear door closed, which is pretty good for a two-seater sports car.

The luggage compartment was covered by Hardura matting (in two pieces on earlier cars, one piece later) secured by 'Durable Dot' fasteners. The two wooden floorboards underneath protected the spare wheel and petrol tank. At first, the rear door came without an electrically heated anti-mist element, but this rather essential piece of equipment was soon offered as an option and was later standardized. Sundym glass also became an option,

Very early E-types had their bonnet louvres contained in separate panels let-in to the main bonnet centrepiece. Within a few months, however, the louvres were pressed directly into the panel itself.

110 mph taking longer than 7 seconds to cover in that gear, and most taking little over 5 seconds. But, rather captivated by the idea of marketing a 150-mph car, the road test cars supplied by Jaguar to such journals as *The Motor* and *The Autocar* were rather well-prepared, and the acceleration and top speed of these cars could not be matched by normal production examples.

One hardly wishes to demolish a tradition, but the truth of the matter is that although the differences in performance were slight, a standard 3.8 E-type is not capable of a genuine two-way 150 mph average, or of a 0-100 mph time of less than 16 seconds. More representative figures would be 143-145 mph at the top-

Originally the E-type's bonnet was secured by a budget-lock, the key for which was part of the toolkit; the escutcheon covering the hole was the same as that used on the Mk V saloon rear-wheel spats. After a few hundred cars were made, internal locking handles were employed which engaged a male bracket on the bonnet and pulled it into a female receiving catch on the bulkhead. This proved essential to stop bonnet shake as such a large expanse of metal was involved.

either heated or unheated, but only for the rear door.

Closed comfort was also offered on the open car in the form of an optional glass-fibre hardtop; whether ordered with one or not, every roadster was temporarily fitted with a 'master' at the factory before it was dispatched to ensure that if an owner subsequently ordered one it would be a respectable fit. Eventually a number of independent firms offered a range of hardtops for the E-type as well, such as Lenham and Heron Plastics.

On the road the E-type had few peers. It was faster than virtually any other production car, yet in most conditions all the power could be used and even in the wet the car was utterly controllable. Despite the relatively skinny 6.40 x 15 cross-ply Dunlop RS5 tyres, the combination of a limited-slip differential and a well-thought-out independent rear suspension enabled the driver to make maximum use of the considerable horsepower at his command.

The engine, of course, was a delight. Even with the 3.07 axle (3.31, or the very high 2.93, were alternative ratios) it would pull smoothly from 5 mph in top, with no 20-mph increment up to

An early fixed-head E-type photographed in 1961. The escutcheon for the bonnet lock is clearly visible, and is about the only item which identifies the age of the car — otherwise the appearance of the E-type changed little from 1961 to 1967.

The 3.8 open two-seater, hood down. Roadster models had a chrome trim-piece running across the top of the door, an embellishment the closed car lacked. Doors are not interchangeable between body styles, although fixed-head doors can be altered to fit the open car, and vice versa, by a craftsman. Typically, this export car is equipped with white-wall tyres.

The same early roadster, with top up; made in Jaguar's own trim shop, the cloth top was well finished, quick to erect and tolerably wind and waterproof. It also possessed a very reasonably sized rear window. Note the slim, neat rear-light units above the long, tapering bumpers; although similar in appearance, these light units differed from roadster to fixed-head, owing to the more gentle shelving of the roadster's rear quarters.

A popular option was the smart glass-fibre hardtop, which suited the car's lines very well. In winter conditions it did, however, tend to emphasize the inadequate demisting arrangements. This early export two-seater has the optional chrome wire wheels — standard finish was stove-enamelled silver. Non-eared hub caps were fitted for German-market cars, and later for the USA. This view also shows the 'long' rear chrome silencers — later these were changed to a shorter style.

30

The hardtop was fixed to the screen by three simple over-centre catches. Note the big, handsome wood-rimmed steering wheel, the large, highly legible instruments, the old-fashioned light switch of prewar origin in the middle of the centre panel, and the slide controls for heater and choke (with black plastic knobs which were inclined to break off). The steering column was adjustable for reach via the knurled ring, and for rake via a lock-nutted slide visible below the rev-counter.

The normal top could be left folded in place when the hardtop was fitted. The leather-trimmed bucket seats of the 3.8 car were not universally popular, but remained, with minor and virtually invisible changes, until the advent of the 4.2. They were not adjustable for rake. Sills were covered in grained vinyl, and the transmission tunnel was topped by a polka-dot-patterned aluminium finisher, matching the console and central dash panel.

A Radiomobile receiver was an optional extra, and was set into the console above the gear-lever pod; a closing panel was fitted when a radio was not specified. Later 3.8 cars had the aluminium on the gearbox cover replaced by a rexine finish.

Luggage space in the roadster was minimized by a very shallow boot, though some additional space for oddments could be found behind the seats. The sprung bootlid was opened by a catch inside, which on the fixed-head operated the rear door. Either a weak catch or a certain lack of rigidity in the open bodyshell could sometimes result in the bootlid popping open if the car was driven quickly over a rough piece of road.

Rolling back the Hardura matting and lifting out a wooden floorboard would reveal the spare wheel and toolkit. The kidney-shaped petrol tank, rubber-mounted to prevent drumming, could be removed after taking out another section of board. The warning notice behind the spare wheel relates to the immersed Lucas fuel pump used on 3.8 cars — a reminder to disconnect the battery terminal before servicing. The arrangement was similar on the fixed-head car.

The E-type's top could be easily managed by one person from a sitting position, and like the hardtop was secured by three over-centre toggle clamps. This view also shows the slim outer door handles, which some people found irritatingly small. The rear-view dipping mirror, mounted on a tensioning rod which ran from dash to the top screen rail, was similar to that used on the XK 150. This 1961 roadster has the rather unusual large-grain-pattern leather, which was sometimes used in early cars.

end, and a 0-100 mph time of around 19 seconds, as was recorded by *Road & Track* in early-1964, when they tried an E-type which presumably had not been 'got at' by the factory.

This exuberant piece of marketing was to have irritating consequences for Jaguar later on, because from then on, to avoid quizzical looks, each successive E-type model produced had to achieve figures which were as good as, if not better than, the 3.8's in the hands of magazine road-test staff. The first 'press' E-type probably not to have been given a modified engine was also the last — the 5.3-litre Series 3 which, in spite of a better power-to-weight ratio, could only just match the original 3.8 figures by *The Motor*.

Not that these differences would have been detectable except with a stopwatch; the production E-type was far quicker than anything save the lighter Ferraris and the muscle-engined Chevrolet Corvettes, and scored over both these in ride comfort and noise suppression. This superiority in performance, together with exquisite looks, put the E-type firmly amongst the world's most wanted cars, and against such a uniquely pure blend of speed and functional grace, minor failings like a slow gearchange, sometimes nominal brakes, high oil consumption and rather cramped accommodation simply didn't stand a chance. To most people, the E-type was the ultimate sports car; and it was going to get better still.

The fixed-head coupe was provided with a generous luggage platform over 4ft long, the only limitation being the sloping rear door, which restricted height. Removal of the floorboards under the two-piece Hardura mat disclosed the spare wheel and petrol tank.

A very famous E-type roadster, used by *The Motor* to achieve almost exactly 150mph early in 1961 during a hectic Continental road test, in which 3,000 miles were covered in just over a week. The stick-on front registration number was a feature of all home-market cars, but abroad a separate numberplate carrier was usually required, and this was fitted below the nose aperture. To prevent it grounding when the bonnet was raised, the plate was eventually linked by a rod to the hinge mechanism, causing it to tilt as the bonnet came up.

While *The Motor* were testing 77 RW, *The Autocar* were trying out 9600 HP, the Geneva Show press-demonstrator fixed-head coupe. Just over 150mph was obtained, assisted by a 'blue-printed' engine — and years later the author discovered (to the surprise of the then-owner) that 9600 HP also possessed other non-standard features such as an aluminium rear door and Perspex side and rear windows, obviously in the interests of weight-reduction.

The more familiar production 3.8 open two-seater with the invisible (interior) bonnet fixing. The original 'stepped hub' wheel of 3.8 and early 4.2 cars can be seen, which was superseded in 1967 by a stronger wheel, also of 72 spokes, but with a redesigned hub-centre and angled-back spokes. The 5-inch rim was retained until the Series 3 cars, however.

By July 1961 E-type production was well under way. This picture shows some 50 E-type roadsters about to be dispatched, under the window of Sir William Lyons' own office (top right-hand corner of the Browns Lane office block).

The 4.2 open two-seater, visually very little different from its 3.8-engined predecessor. This left-hand-drive car has the nose-mounted registration plate and narrow-band white-wall cross-ply tyres. Lights, bumpers and other chrome trim pieces remained as before, although new sealed-beam headlamp units were fitted.

From the rear, too, little had changed, although the shorter rear silencers were fitted. The only real visual difference was the '4.2' badge placed underneath the 'Jaguar' script on the bootlid. Dunlop RS5 cross-ply tyres were still the standard wear, although Dunlop radials were soon to become an option.

CHAPTER 3

Four Point Two

1964 to 1971

It was called the 4.2 E-type when it arrived in October 1964 — the 'Series 1' tag didn't come until there had been a Series 2 to outdate it. Basically, the new car looked exactly like the 3.8 before it (about the only external difference was the '4.2' badge on the bootlid) but it had undergone many changes under the skin.

Its name came from Jaguar's new version of 'old faithful', the twin-cam engine having been expanded for the second time in its production life. Again, the desire had been for more torque to give the saloon-car range better pulling power, from which the E-type also benefitted. The increase in capacity from 3,781cc to 4,236cc had been achieved by increasing the bore size from 87mm to 92.07mm, although to do this the pots lost their equidistant spacings and were 'siamesed' so that the bigger bores could be incorporated in the same size of block.

So while cylinders 2 and 5 were kept in the same place, the two end cylinders — 1 and 6 — were moved outwards, and 3 and 4 were moved closer together in the middle. This assymetric spacing required a new crankshaft, which was also given stiffer webs to strengthen it, and of course the bearing positions also had to be readjusted. Loading on the seven main bearings was lessened by altering the four crankshaft balance-weights, while at the front of the crankshaft was a new torsional damper to break down the torsional frequency of the crank.

The result was an increase in torque from 260 lb ft to 283 lb ft at 4,000 rpm, though improvements to the engine did not stop there. Better water circulation around the chrome-iron cylinder liners improved cooling, while new pistons and rings (fitted to some later 3.8 E-types as well) helped to cut down oil consumption. A better inlet manifold was fitted, giving straighter inlet tracts (thanks to space left by the rearrangement of the brake servo system) from the three familiar SU HD8 carburettors; a one-piece casting, the manifold had a cast-in vacuum balance pipe and integral water rail, which gave a better water flow and complete freedom from steam pockets. Otherwise, the cylinder-head was left alone, even though its combustion chambers now overlapped the staggered bores — which sounds a little makeshift, but in practice made no difference. Petrol was now brought from the tank by a twin SU AUF 301 electric pump instead of by the immersed Lucas pump.

Neither was ancillary equipment left alone. Gone was the dynamo, and in its place was a new Lucas 11AC alternator; this was capable of giving a full charge at only 910 rpm, which was definitely needed — driving for a couple of hours in crawling traffic with lights and fan on could drain the battery of the 3.8 car quite easily. A new starter was fitted, too, of the pre-engaged type, which meant that a misfire would not throw it out of mesh, but would allow it to keep churning the engine round — especially useful in low temperatures. The whole electrical system was also changed to negative earth.

Another change under the bonnet was the disappearance of the bellows servo; instead, a remotely mounted Lockheed vacuum booster was installed. The brake master-cylinder was still attached directly to the brake pedal lever, but on it was a vacuum valve, which transmitted response to the pedal over to the booster, via a dual-line system. Both calipers and discs were deemed adequate so the braking equipment at the wheels remained the same, except that the front discs received dirt shields.

The 4.2 engine looked much like the 3.8 power unit despite its internal differences. The redisposition of the cylinder bores resulted in a lower maximum rev limit (5,000rpm instead of 5,500rpm), but this made little difference to the car's performance as the greater capacity made up any deficit.

Below left: Front suspension and braking equipment at the wheels remained unchanged on the 4.2, though with the dirt shield standardized; the actual disc was also used for the Mk 2 saloon. This picture gives a good view of the front-suspension wishbones with their inner Metalastic mountings. *Below:* One change on the braking system with the advent of the 4.2 E-type was the servo-assistance; a new line-pressure servo, mounted away from the (new) master-cylinders, gave a considerably greater response than the old mechanical system.

Lots of changes inside, the most important being the entirely new, wider and more comfortable seats. The bright aluminium trim had gone, although the dashboard layout was unchanged, and there was a glove box between the seats. The door trim panel still retained the plated rails, which were inclined to break or fall off.

But most welcome of all was the new gearbox. A completely new Jaguar design, it had synchromesh on all forward gears, with inertia-lock baulk rings, and case-hardened single helical gears. Positive lubrication was supplied by an oil pump driven at the rear of the box. In one go, all the criticisms of the old box had been met.

With the all-synchro box came a new Laycock 10-inch diaphragm clutch, which reduced pedal movement by 1½ inches, although a couple of years later Jaguar would revert to Borg & Beck, whose clutches appeared to be stronger. The power was transmitted to an unchanged rear-end, except that ground clearance had been improved slightly by stiffer rear springs — some later 3.8s had spacers fitted under all four springs to obtain the same effect, which was to obviate grounding on bad surfaces taken at speed.

The rack-and-pinion steering was unchanged, and so was the front suspension in principle, though due to new polyurethane seals, servicing intervals for the ball-joints was increased from 2,500 to 12,000 miles. The light-alloy radiator was gone, replaced by a copper one, although the separate header tank remained.

Outside, all remained much the same, with the 3.8's aesthetic if not practical accessories being retained, such as the slim bumpers, small sidelights, enclosed headlamps (but with more powerful assymetric sealed-beam units inside) and small door handles. Inside the car, though, very substantial revisions had been made.

Gone were the 'sports car' bucket seats, and in their place were much more luxurious items with a lot more padding and provision for altering the rake of the squab (although not by that much). A glove box now sat between the seats, and the instrument panel was all-black, the polka-dot aluminium finish having gone for good. The passenger's grab handle received embellishment,

Roadster owners could still take advantage of the storage area behind the seats, a useful supplement to the rather meagre ration of space in the boot. Access to the platform was improved, thanks to the new seats being given a rake-and-tilt facility.

but the more plush rear deck of the fixed-head had lost its little side cubbyholes. The bootlid hinges of the closed model now possessed covers to prevent you squashing your luggage, although these had also been adopted for later 3.8 cars, while the releasing catch for the open two-seater's bootlid now had a lock on it. Armrests on the doors had been a feature of some of the last 3.8 E-types, and these could also be fitted to the new 4.2.

All these features combined to make the E-type a rather more pleasant car to drive, and probably a quicker one, too, although the matter is slightly confused by the rather special road test cars of the period. For most people it was more comfortable, even if the heating and ventilation had not improved and the extra insulation on the transmission tunnel was still insufficient to prevent the cockpit becoming fairly oppressive in warm weather. However, air conditioning was now an established option at £100, although still restricted to left-hand-drive cars. Cross-ply RS5 tyres continued to be original equipment, but the longer-lasting Dunlop SP 41 radials were now approved as alternatives, and would be fitted as standard in the UK by October 1965.

Unsatiated by this considerably more appealing version of the E-type, Jaguar's engineers were determined to widen the car's market still more, and returned to the XK 150 philosophy to produce the 2-plus-2 E-type, which came in March 1966. No doubt they were encouraged in their efforts by pleas from North American distributors, although the new car found favour everywhere because it now made the E-type a viable family car.

For the 2-plus-2 the biggest alterations to the fixed-head shell were the extra 9 inches in length (almost all accommodated by the centre-section and bridged by the much longer doors) and 2 inches in height. These extra dimensions allowed room for the contoured, bench-type seats which were now installed in the rear, and they also gave the necessary additional headroom — of equal importance to the occupants of the front seats, which had been raised to provide foot space underneath for the rear passengers. The rear seats also caused the front panel of the rear bulkhead, which formerly ran across the car directly behind the front seats, to be moved back a little and made shallower. Obviously the glass areas were also increased to make up the height, although the windscreen now appeared rather 'tall' and the door glasses no longer wound down out of sight.

The general level of interior appointment had also been

Left: The 4.2 fixed-head coupe E-type, like the open car, was little different externally from its 3.8 predecessor. At one stage the 4.2 might have appeared with an aluminium bonnet, as a serious feasability programme had been carried out at the factory using this material — advantages would have included a reduction in weight over the front wheels and resistance to corrosion. The factory's experimental glass-fibre shop also investigated plastic bonnets, but in the event the original steel item was retained. *Below left:* The coupe's very useful luggage door, now with covered hinges; the wheelarches had lost their mocquette cloth covering and were trimmed in vinyl, and the platform mat was now one-piece. *Below:* The driver's seat in the fixed-head, which incorporated the same interior changes as the roadster. The centre console still housed the optional radio, with speakers set in the side. The 4.2 cars also retained the big wood-rimmed steering wheel.

In 1966 the E-type range was extended to include a 2-plus-2. The extra height of the car was well disguised, and it was hard to distinguish it from the normal version at a distance, although an aid to recognition was the bright strip carried on the shoulder of the much wider door.

This view tends to emphasize the 2-plus-2's higher roofline. The new car's extra weight and length did not affect handling too badly, though the longer wheelbase increased the turning circle from about 28ft to nearly 43ft.

improved; the criticized heating-and-ventilation system took a leaf out of the S-type saloon's book and appeared with variable-direction outlet nozzles, the tiny glove compartment was given a lockable lid, and a parcel shelf was added on either side of the central console. A hazard warning facility was built into the flasher circuit, and the doors were given anti-burst locks — these were just a preview of the impact which ever tighter safety regulations were destined to have on the E-type.

Thanks to the increased length of the car, the luggage area behind the seats was bigger than ever, especially with the rear squab folded down, which gave an uninterrupted 4 feet 3 inches of space. Mechanical changes for the 2-plus-2 were confined to uprated rear springs to compensate for an additional 2 cwt. Some alterations were carried over to all 4.2 E-types, such as a heat shield for the alternator, wider ratios in the gearbox and a more

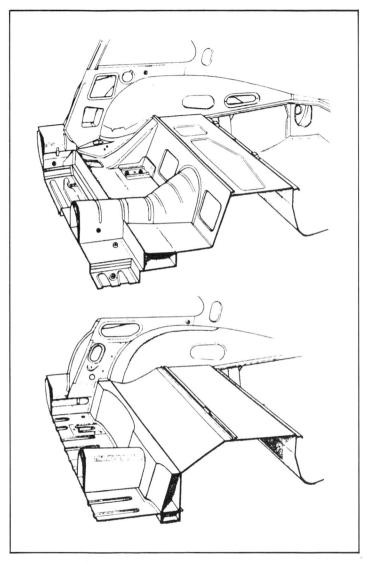

How the extra space for two more seats was achieved — this diagram shows the revised rear-bulkhead arrangement on the 2-plus-2 (upper sketch).

This is what it looked like in practice — the 2-plus-2 floorpan, showing the much lower rear bulkhead on which the two rear seats were mounted. Sound-deadening panels cover most of the floor panels.

comfortably angled clutch pedal.

But it was in the transmission department that another step forward had been taken — there was now room to offer an automatic gearbox, the trusty Borg-Warner Model 8. The E-type adapted to automatic driving better than might be expected, the torquey 4.2-litre engine coping well with only three speeds, even if some 2 seconds was added to the 0-60mph time. The transmission was controlled by a lever on the gearbox cover, which gave the driver some options in D1, D2 and L (low)

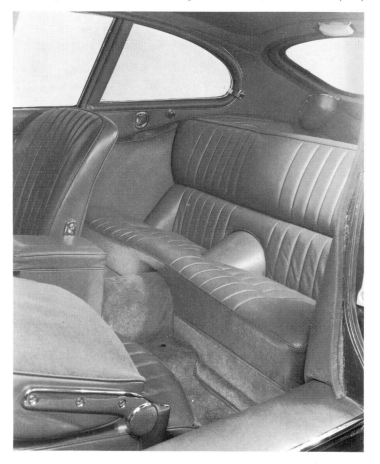

The extended wheelbase of the 2-plus-2 allowed the option (at £140) of automatic transmission. This was the three-speed Borg-Warner Model 8, with D1, D2 and L ('low') positions on the quadrant giving a degree of manual override, besides the throttle-pedal kick-down switch. The transmission fluid was cooled through a heat-exchanger linked to the car's water-cooling system. Note, too, the new parcel shelf, locking cubby-hole and S-type saloon-pattern knobs controlling swivelling outlets, which directed air to the screen or to the occupants.

Right: The interior of the 2-plus-2, showing the new pleated-leather rear seats. If passengers were not being carried the front-seat squabs could be lowered to a semi-reclining position. The 'half-moon' release catch for the rear door can be seen above the wheelarch.

positions, and there was also the usual accelerator-operated kick-down facility.

At first glance the long-wheelbase car appeared visually to be little different from the two-seater E-types, only the higher windscreen with its more upright glass, plus a plated strip running across the shoulder of the door skin, giving it away. Cowled headlights and small bumpers remained. Neither had handling suffered much, with only a slight penalty incurred by the extra weight and dimensions, although top speed showed a drop due to the extra wind-resistance of the taller body — home-market cars with the 3.07 axle just managed 140mph in manual form, while the automatic coupe tested by *Road & Track* with the North American 3.31 specification was reckoned to be capable of 132mph, at which point the rev counter would be nosing into the red band. British automatics had the much higher gearing of 2.88, and *Motor's* example managed 136mph flat-out.

But looming round the corner were much stricter North American regulations concerning such items as the position of

A view of the 2-plus-2 arrangements through the back door. Even with the seat back raised, the platform length was 3ft 5in, and with the squab pulled forward, no less than 4ft 3½in was available for luggage. A versatile and useful high-speed tourer, the 2-plus-2 accounted for almost half of closed Series 1 4.2 E-type production.

The so-called Series 1½ E-type — virtually as the original 4.2 cars, but with open headlights and a few other Series 2 features.

lights, impact penetration, and the toxidity of exhaust emissions — with the deadline set at 1968. These wrought havoc with European imports, killed dead such sports cars as the Austin-Healey 3000, and prevented Morgan from selling in the United States altogether.

We can thus thank the US Federal Government for the Series 2 Jaguar E-type, although some of the changes would no doubt have come anyway. In fact, from the latter part of 1967 quantities of a sort of interim model were issuing from Browns Lane, carrying embryo features of the new model which was yet to come.

Now known colloquially as the 'Series 1½', this car possessed

Interior of a Series 1½ roadster, showing little difference from the normal 4.2, though specifications had begun to vary by this time. On this car switches had not changed to the tumbler type, and there was still the separate starter button.

The same Series 1½ open two-seater of 1967, a well-used press car of the time on which the author recalls putting a good few miles. From the rear, the variant appeared exactly as the previous 4.2 in all three body styles, but was never officially acknowledged as a distinct model by the manufacturers.

The true Series 2 E-type appeared in October 1968, and the changes were immediately obvious — a larger 'mouth' with a fatter decorative bar, headlamps which had been brought forward 2 inches, and larger sidelights relocated beneath the bumpers.

The Series 2 fixed-head coupe, this example showing the flashing indicator repeater lights on the sides of bonnet and rear wings, which were fitted to many export cars and some of the early home-market deliveries. The new type of road wheel can also be seen, with its 'smooth' hub centre.

The 2-plus-2 Series 2 was similarly changed, although a further modification was carried out on this wheelbase, the windscreen slope being increased to further disguise the car's more severe roofline. This car is fitted with the export-type non-eared hub-caps, which were undone by a large ring spanner supplied in the toolkit.

A clear illustration of the windscreen change on the Series 2 2-plus-2 — the pillars remained at the same angle, but the glass was taken out to the forward edge of the scuttle. A beading on top of the facia inside marked the original base of the screen.

Three phases of E-type headlight: *Top*, 3.8/4.2 Series 1; *top right*, Series 1½; *above*, Series 2.

the Series 1 bodyshell complete with slim bumpers in their original position, small sidelights and a nose aperture of unaltered dimensions. It was immediately recognizable, though, because the Triplex glass headlight covers had disappeared. Other detail changes followed later on, including rocker switches and a combined starter/ignition key on the dashboard, and a new cross-flow radiator with twin electric fans.

But the culmination of this development programme was the completely revised Series 2 E-type, announced in October 1968 and displayed at Earls Court, after the hectic development programme necessary to meet all the new Federal regulations. There had been lots of changes.

For the first time since the car's inception there were what amounted to radical changes to the E-type's appearance. Gone were the slim sidelight units and delicate bumpers; new, larger sidelight and flasher units were now in place at the front under larger, raised bumpers, and the open headlights had been brought forward 2 inches. Similar things had happened at the back, with bigger rearlights gathered within satin-finished plinths under the bumpers. Two new reversing lights instead of the original one stood either side of a square (US orientated) numberplate mounting, which meant that the exhaust tail pipes had to be

Series 2 rear quarters — large rectangular light units under the bumper, new numberplate arrangement with bumper continued over the top, repositioned reversing lights and exhaust tailpipes splayed out to miss the lower numberplate. Radial tyres had been standardized by this time.

Inside, a snap-off rear-view mirror was fitted, along with rocker instead of toggle switches and redesigned doors to accommodate stronger anti-burst locks, recessed interior handles and rounded window-winder knobs. New seats which complied with regulations concerning the locking of the squab were installed, plus new seat belts. Although you couldn't see it, the steering column was given a collapsible section to help the car pass the compulsory 30-mph crash-barrier tests (it says much for the E-type's basic construction that no specific structural changes had to be made in order to meet this stringent test satisfactorily).

A new piece of optional equipment which arrived with the Series 2 was Ad-West power steering, chiefly in answer to North American market research. New chromium-plated steel wheels were also offered, though wire wheels with stronger spokes and hubs to cope with ever increasing weight were still the standard fitment.

Another significant change also related to the wheels — for the first time the E-type's brake discs and calipers had come up for revision. These were now made by Girling, and at the front gave a much larger rubbed area through the use of three-pot calipers on each disc. Each caliper contained two smaller cylinders on one side, and a single large one on the other, an arrangement which gave a much more satisfactory pad-area-to-weight ratio.

Other mechanical improvements on the new car were few; the manual gearbox was made yet quieter by a change of helix angle on the gear teeth, and the windscreen wipers were given a more powerful motor. But while home-market and European cars continued with the original triple-carburettor engine in unchanged form, the poor North American owner had to put up with alterations under the bonnet which could not under any stretch of the imagination be labelled as 'improvements'.

Thanks to the geographical peculiarities of parts of California, which retains vehicle and industrial waste emissions in the air and, under sunlight, produces 'smog', it had been decreed that only certain levels of carbon monoxide and unburnt hydrocarbons would be allowed to be emitted by cars — and this ruling was applied to all new vehicles entering the United States, not just those bound for California, although that State was to be generally stricter in its requirements.

At first, recourse was made to the petrol-injection experiments which Jaguar had begun in 1953, but at that time the existing

splayed apart to clear it. Big repeater lamps for the flashers were mounted on each end of the car on the sides for some export models and on very early home-market examples.

Internal modifications were hinted at by the wider aperture at the end of that still-lovely bonnet. Partly because air conditioning was becoming a common option overseas, and partly because the car's cooling system *had* been only marginally adequate, the new cross-flow radiator was standardized, together with two electric fans in angled cowls. Perhaps the only modifications actually to have improved the look of the car, on the 2-plus-2 model the screen-rake angle was increased from 46½ to 53½ degrees by bringing forward the bottom of the windscreen almost to the bonnet, which helped to disguise the high roofline. This resulted in the 2-plus-2 having only two wipers, as there was now insufficient room for a central wiper wheel-box between the bulkhead and the centre of the new windscreen.

Most other changes related to safety and emission legislation.

Series 2 interior, with safety-inspired changes including recessed choke and heater levers, and tumbler switches (which were less reliable than the old type!). The glove box now had a lid and lock. The roadster hood material had already changed from mohair to plastic; open E-types were never supplied with full tonneau covers, incidentally.

equipment could not meter the petrol/air ratio accurately enough to produce the ideal mixture which would leave the least residue in the exhaust. (More recently these problems have been overcome, and now a very successful fuel-injection system is fitted to all North American six-cylinder Jaguars, which in conjunction with larger inlet valves has meant virtually no sacrifice in power.)

After dabbling with air-injection Jaguar's emission engineers finally adopted a proprietary system designed by Zenith-Stromberg, using specially developed Stromberg CD carburettors. At first these used a cross-over system whereby at low engine speeds the mixture was ducted over to the exhaust manifolds, where it was turned into a rather more combustible gas, which could then be burnt in the cylinders with very little unwanted residue. At higher engine speeds a twin-throttle by-pass

allowed a full charge of non-heated mixture to enter the engine.

Later, during 1969, the detoxing system was altered to use a water-heated conditioning chamber instead of the cross-over, where on part-throttle the mixture was warmed and returned to the inlet manifold. At higher engine speeds a by-pass allowed a full flow of non-heated mixture to enter the manifold via a secondary throttle plate. This prevented fuel condensing in the manifold and then finding its way, unburnt, into the atmosphere.

Further refinements added in 1970 included charcoal purification of the petrol vapours given off by the fuel carried in the tank — these were ducted via an expansion chamber to a filtration cannister in the engine compartment, which purged the vapour of impurities before allowing it to enter the carburettors, which in turn were sealed with the float chambers vented into the engine side of the air cleaner. Thus late Series 2 'emission'

Heater controls now included the round chrome knobs for the variable-direction heater/fresh-air outlets adopted earlier on the 2-plus-2 only; formerly, air was ducted through flaps under the scuttle.

Series 2 door handles were recessed into the door panel, and new, less intrusive window-winders were fitted.

E-types do not have vented fuel caps due to the sealed nature of the tank — so don't fit a non-vented cap to a normal tank because you'll get petrol starvation due to a vacuum forming in the tank.

Apart from the emission engineering, further changes to the Series 2 E-type were of a detail nature only. Head restraints were made an option, cold-start ballast resistor ignition was fitted, the previously optional ignition/steering lock was made standard, a partial redesign of the camshafts gave quieter running, and gas-filled bonnet stays took the place of counterbalancing springs; these changes were accomplished during 1969 and 1970.

The edge was certainly taken off the E-type's performance by all the enforced plumbing, and it is doubtful whether the last 'emission' cars (rated at 171 bhp) could manage more than 130mph. It needed the 12-cylinder engine to redress the balance.

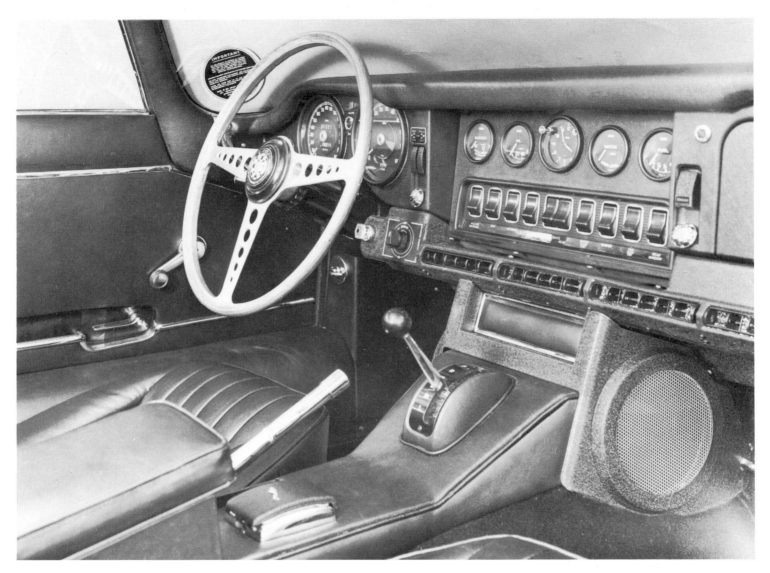

Air-conditioning was quite a common option on export Series 2 cars, but it could not be supplied on right-hand-drive E-types because the steering column got in the way of the unit. This is an automatic 2-plus-2.

Most obvious but least significant change under the bonnet of the Series 2 was the new design of cam cover. More functional were the twin electric fans behind the radiator.

Ultimate indignity? The last North American six-cylinder E-types had the full emission treatment, complete with cross-over preheating and twin Stromberg carburettors. This reduced power output by 30 or 40bhp, and top speed was down to about 120mph. The previously standard limited-slip differential became an option.

Variations on a theme — shortly before the Series 2 appeared Jaguar investigated the contemporary trend towards twin headlights, already used in the 420 saloon of 1966, to see what the arrangement would look like on the E-type. It certainly made the car look wider, but it remained an exercise only, as did the decorative vents seen on this car.

This would have been most interesting, and successful, if it had reached production — the Series 2 long-wheelbase open two-seater, using the floorpan of the 2-plus-2. This configuration was finally used for the Series 3 V12 roadster three or four years later. The more gently sloping Series 2 2-plus-2 screen is used, and with the car's smooth lines (no wheelarch flares like the Series 3) it would have been a handsome and roomy sports car. Perhaps its potential success was the very reason for its non-appearance — it would obviously have affected the sales of the normal-wheelbase roadster.

The experimental bodyshop also produced this updating modification for the E-type, which incorporated a front numberplate in an extension of the bumper running between the overriders — rather similar to the arrangement at the rear of the Series 2 cars. Note also the bonnet badge. Sir William declined to give the go-ahead for these changes.

The most far-reaching revamp of the E-type came towards the end of the sixties, when this extensively revised car was completed in mock-up form. The front-end in particular has received much attention and, with its affinity to the XJ6 saloon, it looks very 'finished'. However, it did not become the 'F-type', and instead the Series 3 and — later — the XJS were to continue the story.

CHAPTER 4

The E-type in competition

International to club events

Nineteen sixty-one, the launch year of the E-type, was the first year since 1950 that no Jaguar was to be seen at Le Mans. It had at last been acknowledged by private entrants that the D-type was just too old for the job, and there hadn't been time for anyone to prepare a new E-type for the event. But while there was talk from the outset of the new sports car treading the path of its illustrious forebear, there was little chance of the E-type emulating the D-type's competition successes, simply because it had been designed first and foremost as a road car rather than one to win races — although that didn't stop one or two people from having a go, as we shall see.

During the E-type's early years it was the Grand Touring category of racing into which the car fitted so far as important international events were concerned. As the name implied the GT class was meant for cars designed for road use in closed two-seater or 2-plus-2 form, with a stipulation (often rather loosely interpreted) that certain minimum numbers were built within the space of 12 months. This distinguished the GT cars from special one-off prototypes and out-and-out sports-racing cars.

The E-type's racing debut was auspicious. On the undulating Cheshire circuit of Oulton Park Graham Hill took on two of the most prominent makes then in GT racing — Ferrari and Aston Martin — and beat them, driving the Equipe Endeavour roadster ECD 400 (850005). Behind him were Innes Ireland's DB4GT Aston Martin, Roy Salvadori in John Coombs' E-type roadster BUY 1, and two Ferrari 250GTs driven by Graham Whitehead and Jack Sears. This was on April 3, 1961.

While almost certainly ECD 400 had a considerably modified engine, it was otherwise quite standard, and the brakes in

First outing for the E-type on a race track was at Oulton Park in April 1961. Here Roy Salvadori in John Coombs' car leads eventual winner Graham Hill in Equipe Endeavour's ECD 400. The grille bar is missing from both cars, and ECD 400 is running without front overriders.

ECD 400's engine compartment, photographed in 1961. The air-cleaner has been removed and ram pipes have been fitted to the carburettors.

particular quickly showed that improvements would have to be made, as the two E-types both suffered from boiling brake fluid, especially on the rear circuit, where the discs were shrouded by the suspension and bodyshell. But this shortcoming did not prevent Salvadori from taking BUY 1 (850006) to victory at Crystal Palace a few weeks later, with Jack Sears in ECD 400 this time to make it a Jaguar one-two in front of the Ferraris.

However, at more important events it was the 250 GT Ferrari which was still on top, as was demonstrated by Stirling Moss at the British Empire Trophy meeting at Silverstone in July 1961, when he beat Bruce McLaren's E-type roadster.

Another 2nd place resulted from the E-type's first excursion abroad, Mike Parkes following Mairesse's 250 GT Ferrari to the flag at Spa, in Belgium. More representative of genuine private owners, though, were Peter Sargent and Peter Lumsden, who took their brand-new E-type roadster to the Nurburgring for a 6-lap race for GT cars before the German Grand Prix. The car was virtually standard but finished 7th, albeit with almost no brakes!

A high proportion of those lucky enough to own E-type roadsters in 1961 raced them. At first, modifications were restricted to cylinder-heads and sometimes brakes, so the cars looked — and were — really quite standard and were driven to race meetings. In this September 1961 Snetterton event, Sir Gawaine Baillie takes the inside line behind Robin Sturgess, their E-types ahead of a 250 GT Ferrari and an assorted field of Lotus Elites and Sprites.

The factory-backed Coombs car, now registered 4 WPD instead of BUY 1, had been receiving a lot of attention, and was running with a lighter (steel) shell and a wide-angle D-type cylinder-head by the time this photograph was taken at Goodwood during the 1962 Tourist Trophy race. Driver Salvadori brought 4 WPD into 4th place in this important event.

In Britain's most important GT race of 1961, the RAC Tourist Trophy, it was again Moss who won for Ferrari, but there were no E-types to challenge him, discretion possibly being the better part of valour by owners of the yet undeveloped Jaguar, who might not have wanted the spotlight on them quite so early in the game.

By 1962 it was possible to perceive a diverging pattern amongst the racing E-types — there were a few very fast factory-prepared cars, and the rest. While Jaguar was never officially to enter an E-type in a competitive event, they were interested enough to give substantial backing to certain private entrants, just as they did in the fifties with such as Ian Appleyard and his famous XK 120, NUB 120. The E-type most concentrated upon was John Coombs' car, 850006.

After the end of the 1961 season the car went back to the factory, where it was dismantled for substantial modifications to

be carried out. These included a new shell built from lighter-gauge steel, saving about 230 lb over the original, an aluminium bonnet which was over 80 lb lighter, Perspex side windows, a competition bucket seat, and a larger-capacity (26 as opposed to 14 gallons) fuel tank.

The engine, too, was more highly developed, although along proven lines using the D-type 'Le Mans' cylinder-head with its larger, re-angled inlet valves, 7/16-inch-lift camshafts (3/8-inch were standard) and triple 45 DC03 Weber carburettors. Stiffer torsion bars and springs were used in the suspension, which also had uprated rubber mountings, while the brakes received larger discs and a new master cylinder and Lockheed servo. Dunlop R5 racing tyres on standard front wheels and the catalogued optional 5½-inch-wide rear wheels provided the rubber.

Appearing with the new registration number 4 WPD, the car was driven regularly at British meetings during 1962, usually by

Dick Protheroe in his first E-type, the fourth right-hand-drive fixed-head built, on the way to a good 6th place in the 1962 Tourist Trophy at Goodwood. The car also won the over-3-litre class in the *Autosport* GT championship that year.

Ken Baker and 7 CXW, one of the busiest club-racing E-types, leading an Elva during the six-hours race at Snetterton in August 1962.

Graham Hill. By this time Ferrari opposition was even tougher as the new GTO had arrived, more or less specially built for GT racing and consequently very light. Hill managed a number of second and third places and the occasional first as development of the car continued.

No major international GT races were entered, though, because it was obvious that the E-type was still not capable of winning important long-distance events as distinct from the sprint-type races on tight British circuits. The only exceptions were home events such as the International Trophy race at Silverstone in May 1962, where Hill achieved a good third behind the GTO Ferraris of Parkes and Gregory, and the TT at Goodwood, where Salvadori finished 4th. But with the Manufacturers' Championship of Makes being transferred to GT racing, elevating its importance and prestige, Jaguar decided to go one step further, and for 1963 they produced several all-aluminium E-types in an attempt to match the Ferraris. The story of the true 'competition' E-types is told in the next chapter.

Meanwhile, 'the rest' continued to have fun. E-types generally were hard to come by in the first months of production, but quite a high proportion of the open two-seaters which did escape the export net saw some kind of competitive motoring. Two of the greatest triers were Peter Lumsden and Peter Sargent, at first with a production roadster, 898 BYR. This car had two very busy seasons, and besides many club races tackled successfully it was entered in some of the 'classics' which the factory-prepared car avoided. These included the 1962 Nurburgring 1000kms, which it failed to finish, and Le Mans the same year where, with the aid of D-type engine modifications and an aluminium bonnet, 898 BYR gained an excellent 5th place overall just behind the factory-prepared fixed-head coupe entered by Briggs Cunningham.

Both Cunningham and the two Peters were later to graduate to fully-fledged lightweight E-types, but these were not to be available until 1963. Even more successful as a private entrant, though, was Husbands Bosworth garage proprietor Dick Protheroe. He had already completed a number of seasons as one

E-types at Brands Hatch, the scene of many a duel. Peter Sargent's lightweight 'E' leaves the start in company with Ken Baker and, far right, the very fast Roger Mac.

Lumsden and Sargent's **898 BYR** at the 1962 Nurburgring 1000kms event, with its slightly odd aluminium bonnet and coupe top. Later in the year it finished 5th at Le Mans, but on this occasion it dropped out with a broken wheel.

of the quickest XK drivers, and turned to E-types on taking delivery of a new fixed-head in September 1961.

Ordered with competition activities in mind, CUT 7 (860004) arrived with a D-type head and triple Weber carburettors already installed and a braking system modelled on that developed for BUY 1/4 WPD. Protheroe had a good 1962 club-racing season with his new car, while also running in more important events such as the 1962 TT, where he achieved an excellent 6th position, a couple of places behind Salvadori in the Coombs car. For 1963 he built up a new fixed-head, substantially lighter than the first car, but this was written-off on almost its first appearance in March of that year. It was rebuilt, only to be outclassed by the new lightweight E-types, although Protheroe was rewarded for his efforts by being allowed to buy an experimental fixed-head E-type from the factory, with special 'low-drag' bodywork by Malcolm Sayer.

Another successful 1962 campaigner was Ken Baker, who also equipped his car with an aluminium bonnet, doors and bootlid, together with a D-type head on the E-type block. At the end of the 1962 season, when the car had scored 19 wins out of 24 races,

Patrick McNally tested 7 CXW at Silverstone for *Autosport* and recorded acceleration figures of 0-60mph in 5.2 seconds, 0-100mph in 11.2 seconds, and a standing ¼-mile of 13.3 seconds. The car was driven on the road, too!

Given one or two monocoque changes, 7 CXW had a long and very active life. A notable owner after Ken Baker was Rob Schroeder, who scored almost as many wins, then, after a short spell in the late-sixties with Alan Minshaw, it was further modified by Ron Beaty of Forward Engineering. With John Harper driving, it then proceeded to dominate the big-engined classes of what had become Modified Sports Car racing in Great Britain, scoring nine wins and 14 second places during the 1971 season. A couple of years later it was written-off by a new owner during a private practice session at Silverstone.

So far as truly international races were concerned, it was virtually only Dick Protheroe who could bring home results for Jaguar, outside the few appearances of the 'lightweights'. Thanks to the efficiency of the low-drag coupe and good preparation, Protheroe achieved a significant second place on the high-speed Reims circuit in the GT race held there in June 1963, with only a

The beautiful lines of Malcolm Sayer's aerodynamic-coupe exercise, based on the E-type roadster. Dick Protheroe used the car to great effect both in Britain and on the Continent, and is seen here winning his class in the 1964 Reims 12-hours race. Down the long straight the car was pulling 6,000rpm in fifth gear, or 168mph.

Protheroe's low-drag coupe, rear aspect, rounding Lodge Corner at Oulton Park during the 1965 Tourist Trophy. The driver in this instance was David Wansborough, who finished 2nd in class to a GTO Ferrari. Sadly, Dick Protheroe was killed in a Ferrari not long afterwards.

Hardy campaigner Warren Pearce, one of the best-known E-type drivers, pictured in 310 WK chasing the ex-Tommy Atkins lightweight 'E' during the Guards 1000-miles race at Brands Hatch in May 1965. Pearce's car underwent continuous development and was always one of the quickest E-types in club racing. However, in this event it was a very standard-looking 4.2 fixed-head which was to uphold E-type honours, Jackie Oliver and Chris Craft taking it to a class win.

The E-type never did particularly well in rallies, but things might have been vastly different had they been the subject of factory preparation, at least until the very rough special stages took over from tarmac. One of the few private entrants was J. Cuff, seen here ascending a Col during the Tulip Rally in May 1962.

The E-type adapted well to the 'Modsports' era of wide tyres, and John Quick's famous blue coupe was always one of the fastest runners until his retirement in 1970. WOO 11 is seen here on its favourite hunting-ground, Brands Hatch, in 1969.

The V12 E-type has never had a particularly outstanding racing career in the UK, though when Production Sports Car racing (for virtually standard road cars) was introduced around 1975 Jaguar employee Peter Taylor did very well and gained some overall victories before cars like the much lighter Lotus Europas were fully developed.

Ferrari prototype ahead of him and all the GTOs behind. So it could be done. The RAC TT at Goodwood the same year netted a creditable 6th place, with Peter Lumsden 9th, while 1964 brought a crash in practice for the Nurburgring 1000kms, but a good class win at Reims again.

However, 1963 and 1964 were the peak years for E-types in international racing, and thereafter, with a few exceptions, their racing activities were confined to club events, where they were to remain ultra-competitive for a good many years. Two of the most well-known club campaigners were John Quick and Warren Pearce. Quick's car, registered WOO 11, came to the track after a short international rallying career, and with a Weslake engine and lightened bodywork it probably collected more awards for its driver than any other E-type racing. Warren Pearce's roadster was its chief rival, and Pearce gained 17 victories during his peak year of 1966.

This record (if it was one) was exceeded in 1967 by Herefordshire driver John Lewis. His ex-David Cunningham, Paul Vestey car won at every circuit in the country except Cadwell Park (which had a 2-litre limit on it) and Lydden Hill (which was not visited). No less than 21 outright victories were scored in 1967, and six lap records taken, while in 1968, being entered in championship and national races only, the car was either first or second wherever it appeared and won the Freddie Dixon award for sports cars. The opposition in those days was composed mainly of Austin-Healeys, Morgans, Triumph TRs, Lotus Elans and some very fast MG Midgets, although in the early-seventies the E-type was more hard-pressed by such as Rhoddy Harvey Bailey's Corvette Stingray and John Cooper's Porsche Carrera.

The occasional 'international' result might still occur, however, and in 1966 John Harper and Mick Merrit drove a rebuilt and largely standard ex-Jack Lambert roadster to Belgium for the Spa 1000kms race, complete with spare tyres on the hardtop roof.

There they managed a creditable 2nd place in the GT class before travelling to the Nurburgring, where on that very testing circuit another 2nd place resulted, with only the works Ferrari 275 GTB of 'Elde' finishing ahead of the E-type, by a bare 2 minutes after 1000 kilometres of racing.

Overseas owners were racing their E-types as well — as we have seen, Briggs Cunningham had entered a factory-modified and lightened fixed-head coupe in the 1962 Le Mans race and finished 4th, having just caught the Lumsden/Sargent car, whose gearbox was failing. The same year he had also achieved a measure of success in the United States running an open two-seater E-type fitted with aluminium body parts, but disregarding some laps during the 1962 Le Mans practice days this car did not appear in Europe. Pherstappem and Rutherhardt won the over-3-litre GT class in the Nurburgring 1000kms of 1963, but against little opposition — the much faster GTO Ferraris were of 3-litres capacity and so ran in another class.

In the United States the most active E-type driver in club events during the sixties was undoubtedly Merle Brennan. His fixed-head ran in the Sports Car Club of America championship, and between 1964 and 1966 the car won 39 races out of the 42 entered. This car was prepared by Joe Huffaker, of Huffaker Engineering Inc., of San Rafael, California, who was later to manage British Leyland's V12 racing E-types on the West Coast of America.

On the East Coast, the E-type saw action with Peter Schmidt competing regularly between 1965 and 1975, and winning the 1974 North American Road Racing Championship. His car was tuned by Al Garz of New York. Also overlapping the entry of the Leyland-backed V12 E-types was the venerable six-cylinder roadster campaigned by Gran Turismo Jaguar of Eastlake, Ohio, which delighted in beating much more modern opposition in C-Production racing, such as the highly developed Datsun 260Zs.

Driver Roger Bighouse also gained the quite rare distinction of winning a National round of the SCCA Championship at Nelson Ledges in 1974, but development continued, and in 1978, with expatriate Englishman Fred Baker driving, the team surpassed itself by achieving a run of no less than 11 straight wins at Nelson

John Burbidge's modified E-type was a consistent winner during the first half of the seventies, and is seen here on its home circuit of Thruxton. The car has since been raced successfully in Scotland by Bob Kerr.

West country driver Guy Bedington tried the hardest to make a race-winner out of the Series 3 E-type in Britain, but although his fuel-injected coupe produced a great deal of power, the car's comparatively great weight ensured that modified six-cylinder E-types were generally quicker.

Ledges Raceway — believed to be the highest total of consecutive victories by any one car at one circuit in SCCA National racing.

Back in England, E-types continue to appear in Modified Sports Car events, although there are fewer competitive cars around now which are capable of beating the much-modified Lotus Elans and Porsches. Active drivers of the past, though, include Ted Worswick, John Burbidge, Keith Holland, Mick Franey, John Filbee, Tony Dean, Brian Spicer, Harry Phillips, Alan Leeson (in a supercharged car) and many others. It was, in fact, quite common to see as many as six or eight wide-wheeled E-types on the grid at Brands Hatch during the late-sixties, but the weight of the car, plus the expense of building a competitive engine these days, has resulted in only sporadic appearances in more recent years.

In North America the E-type had a surprising last fling in up-to-date competition when Jaguar's sales and marketing division in the United States decided to give official backing to two Series 3 V12 roadsters in SCCA racing. Together with Quaker State Oil and Goodyear, they sponsored Group 44 Inc. on the East Coast

and Huffaker Engineering on the West; both these teams had long experience with preparing British Leyland sports cars, and both produced supremely immaculate V12 racers with various modifications as allowed by SCCA rules.

The first season, 1974, went very well with Bob Tullius winning virtually every race in the East and Lee Mueller equally successful in the West. The two V12s met for the first time at the Road Atlanta, Georgia, finals in November, where they came up against the E-type's traditional rival, the 5.7-litre V8 Chevrolet Corvette. But just as in the E-type's first encounter with an earlier Corvette, in September 1961, when E-type driver Bill Krause had to give best to Bob Bondurant's Corvette at Santa Barbara, both Mueller (who retired with a puncture) and Tullius were beaten by the defending Class B Champion Bill Jobe and his Corvette.

But this was no disgrace — as in 1961 it was the car's first season, and there was still much to learn. Both V12s appeared again in 1975, and both had the measure of the opposition. At the Road Atlanta finals at the close of that season Bob Tullius left no doubt as to the superiority of the Big Cat over its American

68

Tecalemit-Jackson fuel-injection on a racing V12 E-type, making the engine compartment look even more complex.

Jaguar's V12 could also be converted to Weber carburation; this is Bill Cole's hill-climb car.

counterparts, and came home a clear winner to gain the SCCA Championship.

This was a fitting end to the E-type's career, because by then the Series 3 was obsolete, too. The Group 44 E-type came home to Britain and is now much admired when on display at Browns Lane or at British Leyland's own collection at Donington Park; the Huffaker car is privately owned. It is certainly pleasant to record that the last E-types to be officially backed proved themselves to be so successful.

It required the efforts of the Group 44 and Huffaker Engineering teams to bring the V12 E-type its major successes, and it all happened in the United States. Here Bob Tullius' championship-winning car blows a tyre during a demonstration match race on the Monterey circuit in 1976, the cars' last active season. Lee Mueller's car (right) is now privately owned, while the Group 44 car was retained by BL and is now back in Great Britain.

Engine compartment of the Group 44 V12 E-type. Ducting takes cool air to the carburettors; the four Strombergs were retained as demanded by SCCA rules.

Six-cylinder E-types can still be competitive in the States, too; this is Gran Turismo Jaguar's roadster, which recorded a string of victories during the 1977 and 1978 seasons in SCCA Class C Production racing, with Englishman Fred Baker taking the car to a record-breaking string of 11 consecutive wins at the team's local circuit, Nelson Ledges, during 1978.

Meanwhile, development of the six-cylinder E-types continued, with this picture showing typical modifications — coil springs instead of the heavier torsion-bars, and a rear-mounted radiator for better weight distribution; an oil-cooler has taken its place at the front.

John Coombs' 4 WPD, the first competition E-type, and a metamorphosis of the original steel-bodied car raced from 1961 to the end of 1962; this picture shows the car at an early Silverstone appearance. The competition E-types always ran with their hardtop in place; these were in light-alloy, instead of the glass-fibre construction of the standard road cars. The vented bootlid allows hot air from the region of the inboard rear brakes to escape.

CHAPTER 5

The Lightweight E-type

Jaguar's dashing dozen

As we have seen, the E-type was not really a match for the very specialized and very expensive Ferrari opposition on the track. Its main virtues were tremendous value for money, effortless performance and a comfortable ride — in other words, the E-type was a highly successful road car, which almost by definition prevented it from being an automatic success on the track, and no thought was paid to this aspect of its potential during its design stages.

But as the factory-backed development of John Coombs' 4 WPD proved, the gap between a modified E-type and the Ferrari 250 GT (then the car to beat) was not *that* great. When it also became known that GT racing would be given the Manufacturers' Championship for the 1963 season, the temptation to 'have a go' proved too great, and Jaguar answered the pleas of keen private entrants like Coombs and Briggs Cunningham by building what they termed the 'Competition E-type'.

The manner in which the competition E-type was built is easy to sum up — simply, everything that could best be made in light alloy, was. The monocoque centre-section was thus duplicated in aluminium alloy, following almost exactly the same pattern as that of the production steel car. The framework holding the engine and front suspension remained in steel, largely because on a weight-for-strength basis steel tubing was more efficient than alloy — a precept which was followed by Jaguar's engineers on later D-types, too.

The brakes and suspension incorporated the lessons learned from racing the rebuilt 4 WPD during the 1962 season. Production-type front suspension was used, but with different mounting points for the wishbones, while the torsion and anti-roll bars were at least 25 per cent stiffer. At the rear, stronger suspension parts from the Mk 10 saloon were used, in conjunction with stiffer springs and a 25 per cent stiffness increase in the rubber mounting blocks holding the (steel) rear-suspension bridge to the monocoque. The braking system received considerable attention, and thicker discs with larger calipers (from the Mk IX saloon) were fitted at the front. The Kelsey-Hayes servo was dispensed with and a conventional line-pressure booster installed.

With the engine came more novelties. Jaguar returned to their E2A experiments and fitted the new car with an aluminium cylinder-block, this time of the usual 3,781cc, not the 3-litres used in E2A. Upstairs was the Le Mans 'wide-angle' cylinder-head with big 2 3/32-inch inlet valves and 1 11/16-inch exhaust valves, and a higher-lift camshaft than ever used before in a competition Jaguar at 15/32-inch. As on the later works D-types, fuel-injection was used, but employing the latest type of Lucas mechanical injection equipment. Lubrication was by the dry-sump method, whereby the oil was held in a large tank separate from the engine, with two scavenge pumps collecting the lubricant from the sump as soon as it dropped from the bearings — this stopped the possibility of oil surge. This most sophisticated of Jaguar XK engines easily gave more than 300 bhp, and in its most highly tuned form could produce over 340 bhp.

The competition E-types were given chassis numbers in the normal sequence of the steel-bodied right-hand-drive open two-seaters, but with an 'S' prefix. Jaguar's delivery book notes them as follows:

The Richards/Grossman lightweight E-type at Le Mans in 1963, the only one of Briggs Cunningham's three entries to finish. Headlights and spotlights were covered during daylight hours.

One of the most successful drivers of lightweight E-types was Roy Salvadori, who was regularly behind the wheel of Tommy Atkins' 86 PJ. Here the car goes through the famous Goodwood chicane as Salvadori drives to 3rd place in the 1963 Tourist Trophy race. Jack Sears, driving 4 WPD on this occasion, chases Innes Ireland's Aston Martin; Sears completed the race in 4th position.

No.	Owner	Delivery	Chassis No.
1	Coombs	15th March 63	S850006
2	Cunningham	4th March 63	S850659
3	Qvale	4th March 63	S850660
4	Atkins	9th April 63	S850661
5	Lindner	7th May 63	S850662
6	Lumsden	May 63	S850663
7	Cunningham	June 63	S850664
8	Cunningham	June 63	S850665
9	Sutcliffe		S850666
10	Jane		S850667
11	Wilkins	Dec 63	S850668
12	Scragg	31st Jan 64	S850669

A couple of other 'special' 'E' types were made about this time, Sir Hugh Ropner taking delivery of a steel monocoque car but with alloy bonnet and competition running gear (S850817), while Pierre Bardinon of France bought a similarly modified fixed-head (S890193).

The recipients of the true lightweights were either Jaguar distributors with competitive leanings, or private owners with established competition records. John Coombs' car, S850006, was on paper still 4 WPD, although in reality, with its new aluminium monocoque, it was a completely different car. It continued in its role as unofficial works development car, driven by an interesting selection of drivers.

The first appearance of the competition E-type was overseas, on the punishingly hot and abrasive airfield circuit at Sebring, where the brand new cars of Cunningham and Kjell Qvale ran in the 12-hours race. Competitions manager of Qvale's British Motor Car Distributors Ltd., of San Francisco, was Joe Huffaker, who 11 years later was to run one of the Leyland-backed V12 E-types.

The new E-type proved to be faster than the Corvettes and more reliable than the Cobras, but could not catch the Ferraris — GT prototypes took the first two places and GTOs the next three, with the E-types (driven by Ed Leslie and Frank Morrell for Qvale, and Walt Hansgen and Bruce McLaren for Cunningham) in 7th and 8th positions.

Graham Hill gave the competition E-type its British debut when he took 4 WPD through pouring rain to win a combined Sports and GT Prototype race at Snetterton towards the end of

Cunningham himself drove car number 16 at Le Mans in 1963, paired with Salvadori, who was unlucky enough to crash after spinning on oil left by Bruce McLaren's Aston Martin.

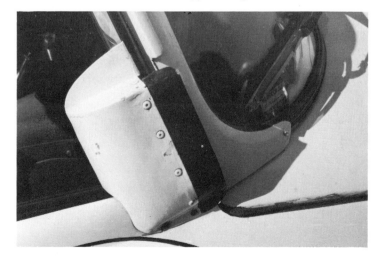

The fuel-injected, wide-angle-head engine of the Cunningham Le Mans E-type. Note the big dry-sump oil tank on the left.

Le Mans detail — fresh air for the driver was provided by this window scoop on the 1963 lightweight E-types entered by Briggs Cunningham.

March. He repeated the success at the Easter Goodwood meeting, with 4 WPD promisingly leading Mike Parkes' GTO from start to finish. Third was Roy Salvadori in Tommy Atkins' car, 86 PJ, which had just been delivered. Parkes and his Ferrari were beaten again by the two E-types at the *Daily Express* Silverstone meeting in May, with Dick Protheroe backing-up the two lightweights with his new acquisition, the Sayer low-drag coupe. Salvadori set a GT lap record, too, at 1 min 42.2 sec, 102.9mph, a time which was not to be beaten in a race by another Jaguar for many years.

But victories on short British courses over 'sprint' distances hardly counted, and the first accurate test of the competition E-type's mettle was to be the 1963 Nurburgring 1000kms. Peters, Lumsden and Sargent took their new car to Germany, and Peter Lindner, the Jaguar distributor from Frankfurt, had accepted delivery of his and had entered it as well.

For the first few laps, it really did look as if the new car had made it — Lindner howled past the pits in the lead as the first lap

Peter Sutcliffe's car at Reims in 1964. The E-type completed the 12-hours race 2nd behind Protheroe's car in the over-3-litre GT class, despite being hampered by a failing battery during the hours of darkness. In 1965 Sutcliffe extended the competitive life of his lightweight E-type by racing it in South Africa.

The superb, businesslike lines of the competition E-type. Note the Dunlop alloy wheels, 15 inches in diameter and secured by a four-peg fixing and knock-on hub nuts, and the petrol filler protruding from the bootlid. The bonnet fixing had reverted to the very early E-type arrangement of outside handles, which were more quickly operated by mechanics during a pit stop. This is Peter Sargent and 49 FXN in its original form at the 1963 Nurburgring 1000kms race, where it held 4th place before leaving the circuit.

The Lumsden/Sargent car in its rebuilt form, with Sayer-inspired bodywork and 'Costin' nose. Note how tyre widths have increased in four years, this picture being one taken at the 1967 Clubmen's Championship meeting at Silverstone.

was completed, ahead of the entire field including Scarfiotti and Surtees in 250P rear-engined Ferrari prototypes, not to mention the GTOs. But while it was not expected that the E-type would keep in front of the prototypes, the disappointment was great when Lindner, holding 4th place, retired through engine failure. Initially, Lumsden and Sargent inherited 4th place, but the car ran out of road on the 33rd lap, so no conclusive result emerged after all. Le Mans was next on the schedule.

Briggs Cunningham entered all three of the competition E-types which ran in the 1963 24-hours race — one was his Sebring car, the other two were driven out from the factory, and all were painted white with blue stripes, the American racing colours. The cars were in trouble almost from the start; Walt Hansgen, paired with Augie Pabst, called into the pits after half-an-hour to complain of gearbox problems, and 4½ hours later Salvadori spun on oil and wrote-off the car he was sharing with Cunningham. Only the Richards/Grossman E-type finished, in 9th place after losing time in another accident.

The next important Ferrari/Jaguar clash was at Goodwood on the occasion of the RAC Tourist Trophy. Salvadori, in 87 PJ, and Jack Sears, with 4 WPD, tried hard but could not catch the GTOs of Graham Hill and Mike Parkes, despite the fact that the E-types were pulling 150mph on the Lavant Straight with the aid of the 'overdrive' top gear of their 5-speed ZF boxes.

A good deal of effort was put into making the E-type more competitive for the 1964 season, including a variety of test sessions, usually at Silverstone with Graham Hill, who complained that the E-type's response to the controls was not quick enough and that the GTO Ferrari was both more responsive and more predictable. Hill's main ambition was to get the E-type set-up really hard, with stronger anti-roll bars and damper settings, and he asked for the steering rack to be mounted direct to the subframe instead of with its usual rubber mounts. Jaguar were also quite aware of the trend towards wider tyres, and Derek White, the very gifted chassis engineer in charge of development, had 7-inch-rim wheels fitted.

Jackie Stewart joined the 'unofficial' works drivers, and during his first practice session at Silverstone, after only 14 laps in the car, he posted a time of 1 min 41.9 sec, which has not been bettered by an E-type to this day. Stewart had cut his teeth on an E-type, racing a slightly modified roadster in his earlier days (registered SSN 1).

The most highly developed of all the lightweights was Peter Lindner's car, on which the factory had really gone to town. Before Le Mans in 1964 it was given a partially new bodyshell with an aerodynamic tail-section developed by Malcolm Sayer on

Prothcroc's car, in which form its drag factor was better than that of the standard E-type coupe, and probably superior to that of the GTO Ferrari. With yet larger valves and a new camshaft, 344 bhp gross was given by the engine, and the car would pull 5,600 rpm in fifth gear, which represented around 170mph.

Lumsden and Sargent took the opportunity of a post-shunt rebuild to modify their competition E-type (49 FXN) on similar lines, from drawings lent by Malcolm Sayer, advice by Frank Costin, and from their own experiments, including driving up the M1 with tufts of wool stuck on the bodywork! Costin's main contribution was the extended nose, which gave better penetration.

Both cars showed up at Le Mans in June 1964 with high hopes. Neither crew expected to achieve anything like an overall victory, because that was the prerogative of the much faster 'prototype' cars such as the Ferrari 275 and 330P, and the new Ford GT40. The primary aim was to beat the rebodied GTOs, the Porsche 904s, and the AC Cobra Daytona coupe muscle-car, all running in the same GT class.

At first, the two E-types ran almost together, around 20th position, but after about four hours the silver car in the hands of Lindner and his co-driver Peter Nocker began to drop back with engine problems. Initially, the Lumsden/Sargent car continued to make good progress and by the fifth hour was up in 12th place, well amongst the GTO Ferraris. Then came disaster when 49 FXN suffered gearbox failure as a bearing gave out. Lindner and Nocker continued to soldier on with an unhappy car until they, too, were forced to retire when the head-gasket blew again, after 15 hours' running. Thus ended the run of the last Jaguar entries at Le Mans.

At home, Jackie Stewart indulged in some spirited driving to achieve a number of places in 4 WPD, and in the Tourist Trophy at Goodwood Peter Lumsden secured a good 5th place in the GT category, ahead of Mike Salmon's Aston Martin DB4GT, two Ferrari GTOs and Phil Hill's Cobra. Sutcliffe also raced his lightweight with success, his best result of 1964 probably being at Reims, where he came 2nd behind Protheroe in the over-3-litre GT class.

The end of the factory's covert backing of the competition E-type coincided with the tragic accident towards the end of 1964 at

Internationally, Frankfurt Jaguar distributor Peter Lindner was probably the competition E-type's greatest exponent, and on a number of occasions he very nearly pulled off a significant victory for Jaguar. At the 1963 Nurburgring 1000kms race he led the entire field, including the rear-engined Ferrari prototypes, for the whole of the first lap, and looked set to demolish the Ferrari GTO opposition until the car's alloy-block engine gave out.

Peter Lindner's E-type, 1964 style. This was the competition E-type in its most developed form, aerodynamically more efficient, and with its fuel-injected engine developing over 340bhp. Here, 4868 WK waits in the paddock at Le Mans; note the addition of spotlights in the nose, faired-in under Perspex covers.

Montléry where, during a 1000kms race, Peter Lindner was killed when his car collided with a Simca-Abarth. The E-type was now definitely outclassed in international competition, especially now that Ferrari was developing a rear-engined GT (the 250LM) — although the authorities refused to homologate it because not enough had been built. The next time Jaguar thought about Le Mans it would also revolve around a mid-engined design, together with the new V12 engine then under development. In fact, the resulting car, the exciting 5-litre XJ13, was never to be raced.

The surviving competition E-types continued racing into 1965 at national level in Great Britain, 4 WPD being sold to Red Rose Motors and, driven by Brian Redman, achieving a good measure of success; this car is now owned by Gordon Brown. Peter Sutcliffe, on the other hand, took his car to South Africa for the 1965 season, competed in eight races and never finished lower than in 3rd position; the car ended up in the United States, a stablemate to Walter Hill's two XKSSs, a D-type and a C-type

and the ex-Dick Protheroe 'low-drag coupe'.

Briggs Cunningham took his two remaining roadsters back home with him, but they were more museum pieces than active racers; they both returned to England in the mid-seventies to enjoy a couple of seasons of competitive 'historic' motoring. One has now gone abroad again, and the other, in company with other exotic Jaguars, is owned by Nigel Dawes. The ex-Atkins/Salvadori car, 86 PJ, resides in Guy Griffiths' museum at Chipping Campden, John Carden owns the Lumsden/Sargent car, though this now has a steel monocoque, as explained, and Bob Jane still has his lightweight in virtually as-new original condition.

Number 12 lightweight, the last to be built, had an active life hill-climbing and won a number of classes driven by expert Phil Scragg; it is now with Nigel Dawes' brother. The car campaigned by Gordon Wilkins, 2 GXO, is on display at the Birmingham Science Museum, while the remains of Peter Lindner's car,

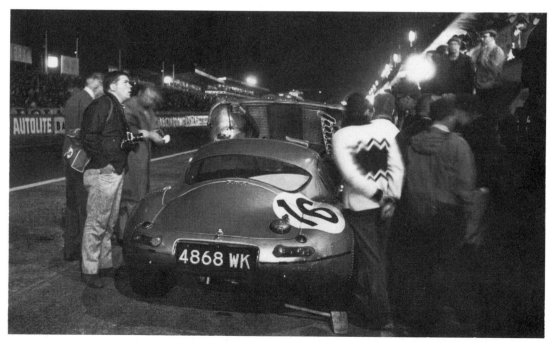

Peter Lindner and his regular codriver Peter Nocker did not have a happy 1964 Le Mans, the newly-rebodied E-type once again suffering from engine trouble — the alloy-block power unit never had the development to enable it to match the legendary endurance of its 3.4 and 3.8 D-type forbears. It lasted just 15 hours and underwent a couple of head-gasket changes — a gasket can be seen clearly in this night-pit-stop photograph.

Bob Jane's competition E-type, probably the only one to be fitted up with such appurtenances as bumpers, overriders and grille bar for road use. This recent photograph shows the car with Jane's production D-type, which he also still owns.

Brian Redman continued to keep the lightweight E-type on the front row of the grid during 1965, even if the events were no longer of international importance. Here the Red Rose Motors car is seen out-accelerating Ferrari and Cobra opposition at Silverstone in October 1965. The XK 120 is Harvey-Bailey's fast ex-works car, JWK 650.

probably the fastest of them all, is in France awaiting a rebuild following many years spent locked up at Montlhéry pending a threatened lawsuit which never materialized.

So the survival rate of competition E-types is very high, and today they are regarded as highly valuable collector's pieces. To drive, they are very different from the road-going E-type and much more akin to the sports-racing D-type, with their very firm suspension and complete lack of noise or vibration damping. In fact, as the writer discovered when trying both 'D' and 'E' on the track and the road, Jaguar's earlier Le Mans contender actually makes a rather more pleasant road car than the competition E-type — although that is hardly a factor relevant to the historic aspects of the car.

In looking back over the competition E-type's career, one inevitably has the benefit of hindsight, and it is easy to say that it should have been built much earlier, in 1961 or 1962, and that the factory should have run the cars itself rather than leaving private entrants to do much of the work. But the car was never more than a sideline at the factory, in contrast to the effort put into the C-types and D-types, and this was revealed when the car came into conflict with the equivalent Ferrari. When it showed the necessary speed it was not reliable, and when it was reliable it was not quick enough; unfortunately, the two qualities never really managed to coincide to produce a true winner.

Some hopefuls expected an all-new F-type to come with the much-rumoured New V12 engine, but instead yet another version of the good old E-type appeared in 1971. New treatment of the wheelarch areas and beefier wheels and tyres gave the coupe in particular a fatter, wider appearance, but most people liked it.

Biggest change at the front was the 'birdcage' grille and an airscoop under the nose. Lights and bumpers followed the Series 2 pattern.

CHAPTER 6

Five Point Three

1971 to 1975

Ten years to the month from the announcement of the original E-type of 1961, the third and last version of the Jaguar 'E' arrived. It had a lot of modern features, a brand new V12 engine of a massive 5,343cc, and a performance which put the E-type firmly back in the 150-mph class. It was also the last Jaguar sports car.

The all-aluminium, 90 x 70 mm, single-overhead-camshaft-per-bank V12 had been developed for the XJ saloon, but had not been ready for production when the XJ was launched in 1968 — this car had to make do (very successfully, one might add) with the old straight-six engine. Then, early in 1971, the new engine was shoe-horned into a rather surprised E-type. The XJ saloon finally received its intended power unit in July 1972, after a year's 'testing' by the public in the sports car had revealed no sinister design faults in the new engine, and after Radford were able to make the numbers of V12s thought necessary.

The new flat-head V12 had its basic origins back in the early-sixties, when Jaguar had a brief and very theoretical flirtation with Le Mans. At that time a 4,994cc racing V12 had been developed, with twin overhead camshafts on each bank and hemispherical combustion chambers — it looked rather like two XK heads angled towards a common crankcase. It produced well over 500 bhp and was installed in the experimental Le Mans racer, XJ13. Road-going versions breathing through SU carburettors instead of Webers were also built, but as time went on the expense and bulk of its design caused it to lose out against a completely new V12 engine which, although less powerful, produced the same or better torque low down and, being simpler, was cheaper and easier to make.

This beautifully smooth unit, over a litre more in capacity than the 4.2 XK engine, produced at the flywheel what the old engine could only manage on paper — 265 bhp or thereabouts. The front subframe of the E-type lent itself to the modifications necessary to enable the car to accept the new engine, and it only required a minimum of beefing-up — namely the addition of strengthening triangular plates to bridge the corners of the upper forward tubes. The bulkhead to which the frame was bolted was also strengthened.

The front suspension remained the same in principle, though the wishbone mountings were angled as on the XJ6 so that nose-dive under braking was cancelled-out by the consequent suspension movement. The vernier system of torsion-bar adjustment was swopped for a cam method, and the suspension uprights now carried big radially vented discs — these ran up to 100 degrees C cooler than the earlier type. Calipers and dual-circuit servo assistance remained much as on the Series 2, though the rear brakes now had under-body ducting to help keep them and the differential cool. Surprisingly, these air scoops were left to the distributor to fit, in order to minimize damage in transit — like the seat belts, they were left loose in the boot for installation during the pre-delivery check.

Outside, the changes were even more obvious. For a start, both open and closed cars now shared the previous 2-plus-2's extended wheelbase of 8 ft 9 in, although the new-length roadster was not given kiddy seats, the space being used as a storage area with a hinged lid. A new type of bonnet was in residence, sporting flares on the wings and a yet larger air-intake, covered for the first time by a grille. The flares were picked up over the rear-wheel arches, again to accommodate the wider-rim — 6-inch instead of 5-inch —

wheels and increased track. Pressed-steel painted wheels with chromed rim embellishers were the standard wear now, with chrome-plated pressed-steel wheels or plated wire wheels of a similar rim width listed as 'extras'. Tyres were Dunlop SP Sport ER 70VR 15 radials, with the option of a narrow-band whitewall. Both roadster and 2-plus-2 now had only two windscreen wipers, though the arms were still not interchangeable as those on the 2-plus-2 were longer.

Internal dimensions had not changed much, being limited by the structural sills on either side, but all of the cockpit floor was now at the level of what previously were the footwells. The 2-plus-2 seats were given more recline adjustment, with the operating lever extended so that it could be more easily reached by rear-seat passengers who wanted to climb out. Also, the seats on the closed car were raised to take further advantage of the higher roof-line, which improved forward visibility and gave greater thigh support — it is probable that over a long journey the 2-plus-2 is a less tiring car than the roadster.

The fresh-air and heater system was improved, although it still

Rear-end treatment was again similar to that of the Series 2, though the registration plate was now mounted on a satin-finish plinth and the bootlid carried a distinctive 'V12' badge.

The heart of the new E-type was the magnificent V12 power plant. The choice of this cylinder configuration was partly for prestige reasons (Ferrari and Lamborghini used V12s) and partly because 12 cylinders give the ultimate in smooth running. This view shows an early-1971 car; from early-1972 onwards visual changes included a simplified cowling over the Marston vertical-flow radiator, repositioning of the coil and ballast resistor in a cooler situation at the rear of the engine, and a simplification of the water plumbing over the engine.

The V12 was Jaguar's first production engine to have an aluminium-alloy cylinder-block; the capacity was 5,343cc (326 cu in), but planned reserves meant that this could be increased to well over 6-litres should the need have arisen, though with the current trend towards ever more economical engines, this development is now most unlikely. Note the chain drive instead of the more fashionable belts, used because of Jaguar's experience with chains and because they helped to reduce the overall length of the engine.

lacked both true effectiveness and simplicity of control; by 1971, cars were being built around heating and ventilation units, so the poor old E-type could not really compete with modern competition on that score.

While the general layout and interior appointments were similar to those of the Series 2, a new smaller 15-inch Springall steering wheel was in evidence, finished black to match the facia. Power-assisted steering was no longer an extra — you had to have it whatever your thoughts were on the subject. Steering kick-back was reduced by better rack mountings, which managed to combine that attribute with less compliance. The roadster version, now that it had the long-wheelbase configuration, could be further tamed by the option of automatic transmission, which was now the improved Borg-Warner Model 12. Otherwise, you were given the still very good Jaguar four-speed manual gearbox in unchanged form, albeit driving through a larger-diameter

clutch.

Alongside the new V12, a six-cylinder Series 3 was also announced, though only about four were made, all fixed-heads. The Series 3 4.2 had all the refinements of the V12, but was powered by the Series 2, full-emission XK engine with Stromberg carburettors and cross-over inlets. This was still supplied in 9:1 compression-ratio form for the home market, with which it was rated at 171 bhp (DIN). Only one appears to have survived outside the factory, and although by all accounts it is a pleasant touring device, with 30 cwt propelled by 171 restrained horses it could only have about the same performance as an XJ 4.2 saloon.

The V12, on the other hand, was a very fast car. The lighter (28.8 cwt) roadster could reach 60mph in 6.4 seconds, 100mph in 15.4 seconds, and achieve 146mph with the 3.07 axle fitted for the British market. The 1 cwt heavier fixed-head took about 7 seconds to reach 60mph, with 100mph coming up in 16½ seconds. At higher speeds, the increased frontal area and drag caused by the larger 'mouth' and flared arches combined to make the Series 3 a less efficient car than the 3.8 or Series 1 4.2, so its ultimate speed was not much more than that of a genuinely standard early car. In practice, the V12 was the quicker vehicle on the road, though, and thanks to its wider tyres, roadholding was improved. Petrol consumption inevitably rose, however, and averaged around 14mpg; at best, a long journey with a gentle right foot might produce 17mpg.

Not that the supremely smooth V12 engine automatically

The use of flat heads on the V12 after decades with hemispherical combustion-chambers was decided upon because of the ease of machining, and because after considerable experimentation this cylinder-head was found to give excellent power and torque outputs in the range from 500 to 4,500rpm. As the ultimate destination for the new engine was the XJ saloon this was an important factor, and it certainly endowed the E-type with an impressive degree of flexibility and top-gear acceleration.

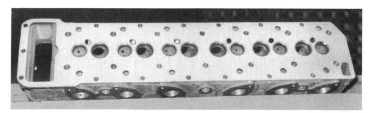

rectified all the E-type's old faults. Heating and ventilation were still not up to the best modern standards, even with a larger heater matrix and heat regulation by a Ranco thermostatic valve, which stopped a sudden gush of hot air when the car was brought to a halt at lights. From about March 1972 the fixed-head, and the roadster when fitted with its new and larger glass-fibre hardtop, were given a measure of full-flow ventilation, together with cold-air footwell vents, but these were merely improvements as a total redesign would have required a new car. The minor controls could still cause confusion, while in more fundamental matters such as ride comfort the E-type was dropping behind such admittedly more expensive rivals as the Mercedes 450SL.

The V12 E-type was at its best as a long-distance, high-speed tourer. There were few cars which could match its top speed and 120/130mph crusing ability, even amongst the exotica from Italy, and none at all the silence and smoothness of its engine. This was in spite of the inevitable loss of power caused by the detoxing arrangements, which were applied to all cars whatever their destination after the end of 1973. These centred around the four Zenith-Stromberg 175 CD 2SE carburettors, and a new (to Jaguar), air-injection system. This used a rotary vane-type pump driven by a vee-belt off the water-pump pulley, which pushed air via a check valve and individual air-injection pipes into the exhaust gases just downstream of the exhaust valves to promote the more thorough burning of the exhaust gases. Again, a sealed system was used on the fuel supply to prevent evaporative emissions, and coincidentally a return was made to a recirculatory fuel supply, with the SU type AUF 406 pump providing a constant pressure of 1½ psi to the carburettors.

There were to be few major engineering changes to the Series 3 E-type during its lifetime, though quite early modifications related to the OPUS transistor ignition, the first of its type to be used on a true production car. This contactless system was highly satisfactory in principle, but owners began to blame it for the niggling misfire at higher engine rpm from which V12 E-types occasionally suffered. Often it was simply the sooting-up of the spark plugs in heavy traffic, which a good fast run would soon cure, although the plug specification was changed from Champion N9Y to N10Y. Many owners claimed they achieved even better results by fitting NKG BP5 ES plugs instead.

In attempts to cure a more persistent misfire, it was discovered

Front view of the V12 showing the four Stromberg 'emission' carburettors with their long inlet tracts curving over the camshaft covers — not an ideal arrangement, but no British-made downdraught carburettors were available. Transistorized ignition nestles in the centre of the 60-degree 'V'. Because of North American emission requirements, the compression ratio went down from 9:1 to 7.8:1; in 1974 home-market cars were also burdened with the full emission equipment, including the air-injection pump.

that the rotor-arm could become porous and thus quickly lose its insulative properties, so this was modified, followed by different plug leads and an uprating of the output voltage from the coil. Small changes were also made to the OPUS system itself, including to the distributor pick-up transistorised amplifier, but in general it worked well and cut out a lot of necessary — and unnecessary — tuning and adjustment. Later amplifiers, coils and ballast resistors were, incidentally, identified by stick-on labels reading 'High Load'.

Some other changes of a less satisfactory nature came early in 1974 in response to stricter US Federal Government regulations. The nose of the E-type suddenly sprouted two overgrown rubber overriders, which did nothing whatsoever for the car's looks.

This view shows the extensive use of aluminium in the V12 — excluding transmission it weighed a modest 680 lb. The engine illustrated here is mated to an automatic gearbox, a similar unit to that used on the XJ saloon, but uprated through the use of an extra large front servo and an additional plate to the rear clutch in order to cope with the increase in applied torque and the higher engine speeds envisaged with the sports car.

Made of a deformable material and secured to the front subframe by strong tubes, they met the letter of the law by preventing damage in a 5mph barrier-collision test. They were not much good when an object was struck from an angle, or when the colliding article had knobs or protrusions, as cars often do, because they were not full-length bumpers, but they did allow the E-type to be marketed in the United States for another year. The new overriders were not offered in Great Britain — Jaguar stated that they spoiled the look of the car and would increase its price; one could hardly argue against either point.

At the same time, USA export cars were also fitted with large rubber rear overriders, and the rear of the car was altered to include a large pressed-steel box-section within the monocoque. The purpose of this box was apparently to distribute a rear impact over the whole of the rear section.

Although more Series 3 E-types were made during 1974 than in any other year, the end was in sight. It was still a great sports car, but there was little more scope for improvement left in the outdated shell, which by the standards of modern body engineering was also becoming expensive to produce. The rest of the world had caught up with the E-type and it was beginning to show; there was now a certain reluctance on behalf of North American customers to pay for a car more expensive than the Corvette, and one which had been more or less written-off by the influential magazine *Road & Track* as being outdated and outclassed. Certainly, for the first time it required an active and aggressive advertising campaign to sell the E-type, which could now be delivered from stock by most dealers.

Manufacture of the closed car had, in fact, ceased by the autumn of 1974, and the two-seater was not long to follow. However, there was still new stock to be sold, and so the announcement of the E-type's obsolescence was not made until February 1975. This left a gap of some seven months before the XJ-S was launched, and maybe, if people had realised that there was not to be a new open two-seater Jaguar, the last remaining E-types would have been sold a lot more quickly.

Underside view of the installed V12. The oil filter is mounted at the front of the engine, behind which is the water/oil heat-exchanger inlet — this arrangement serves the dual purpose of rapidly warming-up the engine oil and controlling its temperature thereafter. Note the triangulating plates on the car's subframe, part of the beefing-up measures taken for the installation of the larger engine.

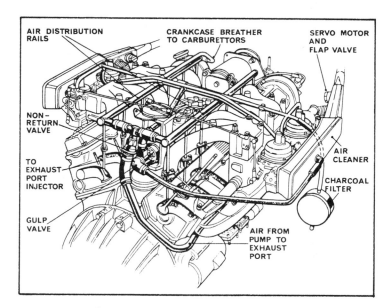

To meet United States emission regulations it was necessary for the V12 to be equipped with an air-pump, which would feed air into the exhaust ports at specified times to help clean-up the exhaust gases. The fuel-supply circuit was also closed, with air from the carburettor float-chamber vents being charcoal-filtered; crankcase fumes were ducted to the carburettors.

The E-type was still cheap, too, as Sir William Lyons' long-term costings had ensured that in real terms the price of the E-type from 1961 until 1975 remained much the same. Towards the end of its production run you could buy a brand-new V12 open two-seater for a total of £3,812 on the home market, compared with £6,249 for a Porsche 911 Coupe, £9,998 for the Aston Martin V8, £6,620 for a Ferrari 246 Dino Spyder and £8,598 for a Mercedes-Benz 450SL coupe — and the E-type was the fastest of them all. The last 50 E-types were finished in an appropriate black, with dashboard plaques signed by Sir William Lyons signifying the fact — bar one, which was painted green to the owner's special order. Most of these cars went abroad, although Jaguar themselves have kept the very last E-type, IS 2872, body number 4S 8989. It remains to this day in the entrance hall at the Browns Lane factory, in company with a yellow Series 1½ roadster, to mark the closing of an epoch in Jaguar's history.

Initially, a six-cylinder Series 3 E-type was catalogued, but only about four were built, of which only one example seems to exist in captivity. All had the full-emission XK engine of the last Series 2s, which looks a little lost in the widened Series 3 frame.

The longer 2-plus-2 wheelbase was standardized for the Series 3, and there were only two models — coupe and roadster. You could, however, order a glass-fibre hardtop for the open car. Wire wheels were now an extra, as in the days of the XK.

The open car adapted very well to the longer wheelbase and was undoubtedly the best-looking of the Series 3 E-types. The space left by the absence of rear seats was given over to a storage area of generous proportions; this and the hood were covered by a short tonneau when the top was lowered.

The two-seater still looked good with the hood up. The narrow-band white-wall tyres were an extra, and you could also order quartz-halogen headlights, an electric aerial for your radio/tape unit, a Bray engine-heater and special metallic silver-grey paintwork at an additional £100 (in 1972).

The roadster's profile was helped by the adoption of the 2-plus-2 screen-rake angle. This export car displays repeater flasher lights (although these could be ordered as an option on home-market cars) and the standard bolt-on steel wheels.

Export roadster interior, with air-conditioning unit in place over the console; this extra could not be fitted to right-hand-drive cars because the blower pump sat in the uppermost part of the right footwell where the steering column ran. Head restraints were mandatory in some overseas countries, but were an extra on home-market cars.

Interior of a pre-1974 coupe with the Series 2/S-type saloon air-distribution knobs, which later were changed from serrated-edge to a design with raised projections. The console containing the radio was a vacuum moulding, and it also housed the cigar lighter, which had been moved from the dashboard. The seats now had a bar adjustment. If you specified a tape player unit you lost the parcel shelf in front of the passenger.

The frontal apsect of the Series 3 was rather more complicated than its predecessors and not everyone liked the grille which hid the four-row vertical-flow radiator; the latter was canted forward to miss the bonnet. With the new duct underneath the nose Jaguar banished any marginal tendency for the E-type to overheat in traffic. Automatic models had the transmission fluid cooled by an additional heat-exchanger mounted under the water radiator and cooled by air from this duct. The grille on the rear door (far right) gave some through-air ventilation. The four-outlet 'fan' exhaust was later changed to twin-outlet, partly because it usually rusted through within six months! This view also shows the wider track of the Series 3 cars — increased 3¼ in at the front and 4¼ in at the rear.

One of the few 4.2 Series 3 cars undergoing emission tests on a rolling road, from which the exhaust gases are being collected and analysed.

The interior of the automatic Series 3 coupe; a perforated-leather finish was used on the seat cushions, and Ambla elsewhere. Gone was the big traditional wood-rim steering wheel, replaced by a leather-rim item with aluminium spokes.

The well-finished rear-seat area of the coupe. Speakers for the radio were positioned under the rear side windows (in the roadster they were mounted in vacuum-formed rear-quarter panels). Seat facings were in leather and non-wearing surfaces in Ambla. Kangol or Britax inertia-reel belts were extras, as was Sundym glass.

To meet USA '5-mph impact' regulations the E-type was fitted with these Nordel deformable overriders and complementary reinforcement of the rear-end. These unattractive additions were not available on home market cars. This picture also shows the later twin-pipe exhaust.

A brave private attempt at rebodying the Series 3 E-type was made by Bill Towns, with sponsorship from Guyson. A couple of these 'Guyson Jaguars' were completed, the glass-fibre panels merely being cladding over the standard steel shell, except for the bonnet, which was completely new. Towns, designer of the DBS V8 Aston Martin shape, also produced plans for a genuine full-flow heating-and-ventilation system for the E-type (including the six-cylinder models) but no-one took it up.

A 1974 roadster with Nordel overriders front and rear.

Last of the line — the penultimate E-type comes together at Browns Lane, with the very last car on the ramp behind it. The last 50 right-hand-drive roadsters were finished in black, except the last but one pictured here, which was painted dark green to special order by the purchaser, Robert Danny (who still has the car). Perhaps because people were waiting for the expected F-type, these 50 cars were slow to sell and were offered by some dealers for as little as £3,500 during 1975.

What the F-type was not to be — a mid-engined road car based on this XJ13 prototype sports-racer built by Jaguars in the mid-sixties as a possible Le Mans contender. Instead, the XJS appeared, to set new standards of comfort, ride and silence, combined with all the speed of the old E-type.

Jaguar's first V12 was this four-cam unit built for the proposed Le Mans car; it developed more power than the production unit which eventually was used for the Series 3, but only at the cost of revs, noise and bulk. This is the injected unit in the XJ13 — road versions were to be fitted with carburettors.

CHAPTER 7

Buying an E-type

The choice, the examination and the test

With three engines and three distinct body styles it can be said that there's an E-type for everyone; certainly the three 'Series' made between 1961 and 1975 offer enough variety in terms of specification and character to suit most types of sports-car driver.

So before you start looking for a car, decide which sort of E-type you want. The original 3.8 E-type of 1961-64 could be called the most historic, being the first of its kind and the beginning of a legend — make sure you're willing to put up with its slow, graunchy gearbox, brakes that are merely adequate, possibly uncomfortable seats, a baking hot cockpit in summer (especially the fixed-head), and a more difficult spares problem.

No? Then consider perhaps the Series 1 4.2, in production from 1964 until 1967. There, you have all the 3.8's slim-line good looks, with the small bumpers and covered headlights, but you can enjoy a splendid, all-synchro gearbox, better seats and a much-improved braking response, with no sacrifice in performance. The power unit in the E-type is virtually as tough as the 3.8; the only reason for a lower rev limit on the dial was to prevent steady-speed cruising above 5,000 rpm, which might just, under highly unusual and unlikely circumstances, coincide with a frequency vibration period in the crankshaft, which could result in damage. I have never come across this in practice, though if the rubber-bonded crankshaft damper fails, it is true that the 4.2 engine will rapidly destroy itself.

The 4.2 E-type also brought the extended-wheelbase 2-plus-2 model, introducing the option of automatic transmission at the same time, which gives the potential E-type owner yet another brace of specifications from which to choose. With the 2-plus-2, you can extend the use of an E-type as an only car until your children are seven or eight years old and have grown legs, and if you choose the automatic version, hours of traffic driving (if that's what you have to do) becomes far less wearing.

Not that snags don't remain — cockpit insulation had not improved very much, nor had the heating/ventilation system, while engine cooling itself could be marginal under certain conditions of climate and traffic. Fast night driving was still not on, because of flare and scatter from those aesthetically beautiful glass headlight cowls.

So if you want greater practicality, move on to the Series 2 E-type, or its rarer cousin, the '1½', of which a surprising number seem to be on British roads; as we have seen, the latter car kept all the neat Series 1 features externally, except that it had much more practical 'open' headlights, and some further refinements internally like the better cooling system and the more modern interior. Maybe worth searching-out.

With the Series 2 proper, it is a question of sacrificing ultimate performance for greater comfort and usability. Whether you can tolerate the big 'mouth', the rather intrusive sidelights and the heavy-handed treatment of the rear-light clusters is up to you, but otherwise it's a matter of deciding whether losing a couple of seconds from the 0-100mph time is worth the undoubtedly better levels of comfort and every-day-use practicality which the car offers.

You can even combine these creature comforts with all the old 3.8's performance, and more, by choosing the Series 3 E-type. The V12 engine is a magnificent replacement for the still not outclassed straight six, and it gives the widened Series 3 a turn of speed which is still unsurpassed by many of today's production

101

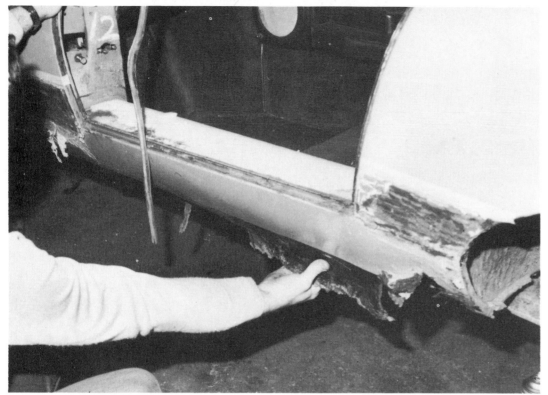

exotics. Time has shown that the V12 is equally as long-lived as the XK power unit, and just as strong. It uses more fuel but although the Series 3 is certainly the best all-round car for serious motoring, few people will buy it now as an every-day machine, and so should not cover the sort of mileage which could make its 14mpg thirst an embarrassment.

But if you have been used to good-quality modern cars, don't expect even the Series 3 to be perfect, because it isn't. It remains a basic design that is approaching 20 years old, and the ride is no longer superb, nor is the insulation from road noise. The hood will not necessarily be rain-proof (particularly at the front rail), while Jaguar never did get the heating and ventilation right, nor the placement of minor controls. Neither does the car feel quite as

rigid and rattle-free as the best modern European sporting machinery. Still, you cannot buy anything practical that is a great deal faster, and a healthy Series 3 can still put 120 miles into the hour on a continental motorway without drama.

Of course, price comes into all this, and with the E-type it is not a case of the oldest being the most valuable. Series 3 cars fetch the most, given reasonably low mileage and good condition, while the value of all other E-types is now more dependent on condition than age. Open cars of all types are more expensive than closed versions, and 2-plus-2s are marginally cheaper than their two-seater equivalents — especially in automatic guise, which can make a Series 1 or 2 2-plus-2 automatic one of the best buys in E-type motoring.

You will soon get an idea of current prices for each sort of E-type by regular perusal of the magazines whose advertisement pages carry a bias towards older cars — *Thoroughbred & Classic Cars, Motor Sport* and the humbler but often rewarding *Exchange & Mart* are notable examples in Great Britain. Don't ignore your local paper, though, where prices may be slightly lower. The biggest selection of E-types for sale are V12s or six-cylinder open-headlight cars — 3.8s and Series 1 4.2s are now rapidly disappearing from every-day use and have to be searched for carefully.

You will find there is an enormous price range, especially amongst the six-cylinder cars, with sometimes a differential of 10 to 1 or more for two cars of the same year. It is purely condition which causes this, and while you may think that the very few top-price-range cars are expensive, always remember that it may take even more money than the price difference to bring a much cheaper but really bad car up to the same sort of standard — and

even then it might not be quite as good as a genuine, original low-mileage car, which will have retained that authentic 'factory' air about it.

In order to value any car you have to be sure of its true condition, and here, rust in the bodyshell is by far the biggest enemy of E-types. As you may have read in Chapter 1, the E-type's centre-section is made up of many quite small panels welded together to form any number of closed-in box-sections; it is these that rust, from the inside outwards, due to moisture being trapped inside.

The trouble is, an E-type is quite easy to repair superficially with glass-fibre and plastic filler so that it looks rust-free. So beware of a recently painted car, and remember that there is virtually no such animal as a pre-Series 3 E-type without rust somewhere, even if it hasn't travelled more than 20,000 miles; not alas, that you're very likely to find such a highly desirable beast as that.

Check where the sill joins the footwell and around the small square jacking points.

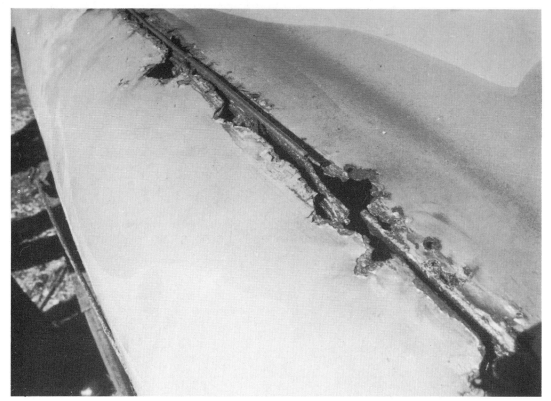

On the bonnet, the wing/centre-section flanges are vulnerable and rust is usually indicated by bubbles in the paintwork along the chrome beading, or underneath by obvious decay in the flange. This is a very extreme case of rot in a Series 1 bonnet.

As for where E-types rust, it is fair to say that most are now old enough to rot through almost anywhere, but you can start at the bonnet. The main danger area, because it is almost impossible to repair properly due to its double curvature, is where the outer wing and bonnet centre-section meet. Poke the flanges from underneath with a screwdriver, and look carefully along either side of the chrome beading on top. Any sign of paint bubbles here usually indicates serious trouble.

Take a good look at the E-type's vulnerable snout, too — the top panel of the nose does not often rust, but dents may have been filled, so feel inside it and examine the underpan area carefully for rust holes, especially around the bonnet-hinge mountings. The bulkhead around the headlamp bowls is also susceptible to rot.

However, do not necessarily write-off an otherwise reasonable car because of a poor bonnet — at the time of writing, at least, you can still buy them from Jaguar and, considering they account for almost a third of the E-type's bodywork, they are a very worthwhile investment.

While you have the bonnet open, examine the engine subframe; look for badly repaired tubing, which may be the result of previous accident damage, and search for cracks at or near joins, particularly on the bottom frame-member on either side. Also, see that no-one has damaged the radiator or surrounding area by trying to jack-up the car on anything other than the main tubular cross-member which forms the bottom arm of the square in which the main subframe ends.

Now we come to the E-type's centre 'tub'. The obvious starting place is the big hollow sills, which may well have been replaced at least once in the car's life. To see if the job has been done properly, and to search for any rot, examine the point where the sill joins the floor underneath the car, and where it joins the rest of the body on either side of the door aperture. Look carefully at the area where the sills project forward of the front bulkhead to carry the air-cleaner on one side and the battery tray on the other. Rot is often to be found here, including in the bulkhead itself, where a particular danger spot is the lower front subframe attachment point — especially on the battery side, where acid can leak out and aggravate the problem.

Outer sill replacement is not difficult, but it rarely stops there because very often the inner face of the sill, where it joins the floor-pan, will have gone, too. So remove the carpets from inside, and try to determine the condition of the metal where the sill meets the floor. Take a careful look at the floor itself while you're there, and be especially thorough if the carpets are wet, because this may indicate holes.

Rot can also occur in the scuttle-section where it meets the sill each side of the car, and in the 'dog-leg' windscreen pillar supports (look upwards from beneath). But a make-or-break point on the E-type occurs towards the rear bulkhead behind the seats. As described in Chapter 1, this has as many as five separate box-sections built into it, each side, all of which can rust, but most important is the mounting point for the radius-arm from the rear suspension. Look from underneath the car for cracks, holes or crudely welded plates — they can all spell trouble, as the vitally necessary repairs can take many hours of skilled work to do properly.

On closed E-types the outer rear wing forms an internal water trap where it joins the inner wing (open cars do not have this arrangement). This results in rot occuring all round the wheelarch and just below the leading edge of the rear bumper. A screwdriver will reveal the structural condition of the inner wing, and you should also be able to feel a clean, single-thickness rebate of metal all round the arch; if you cannot, it probably indicates filler hiding rust damage. If you can take the wheel off, look at the arched box-members which carry the rear-suspension mounting blocks; in severe cases, these can also rust.

On open cars the hood arrangements are such that water can penetrate the wood on to which the hood is mounted, and this can cause the metal surrounding the cockpit to rot. Also, roadster rear wings can rust through on top, so check the surface for bubbles or repairs. Doors on all models should be checked, as they rust through where inner and outer skins meet, a couple of inches up from the bottom. They can also go where the window-frame anchors, and on the horizontal surface which lies beneath the bulkhead when the door is closed.

The last area to look at is the spare-wheel well — likely spots for

Inside the bonnet, poke the dirt away from around the headlight bowl and flanges to determine the condition of the metal.

Rot where the engine subframe joins the front bulkhead is serious — this is a repaired mounting on an early car, and the air-cleaner drum usually occupying this spot has been removed. Normally, access can be gained from underneath.

rust are around the edges of the well and where the strengtheners are spot-welded to the floor. Unfortunately, the petrol tank hides half of the floor, but rot can often be spotted from underneath. The panel between the bootlid and the numberplate area can rot, too, so that is also worth a check.

Interior condition is important on an E-type as retrimming in leather is expensive, and anyway, on Series 1 models some of the original vinyls and mocquettes are unobtainable. You will be lucky if you locate a 3.8 with seats which do not require new leather, but on later models, try to choose a car with seats that are not cracked, torn or holed. Do not be impressed by new carpets, because they are the simplest item to replace on an E-type!

It may not be particularly cheap to recondition an E-type mechanically, but unlike the bodywork, at least it is a known quantity. So while the health of engine, suspension and brakes is obviously important, these items rank second to bodywork condition as a determining factor in the purchase of an E-type.

The six-cylinder engine, in any form, is a tough old lump, and provided the oil pressure is at least 40 psi above 3,000 rpm, there isn't a big cloud of smoke when accelerating hard after a gentle half-mile in top, and the engine feels lively and responsive, the chances are that it will be good for another 30,000 miles or so. Danger signs are smoke and excess oil fumes from the engine breather-pipe, and noise from the bottom timing chain, which is harder to replace than the top chain. A new or rebuilt XK engine is good for well over 100,000 miles if the oil is changed regularly, and mileages of a lot more than double this are not uncommon on the same set of bearings. Noise from the cylinder-head might just be badly adjusted tappets, but if the tapping noise is excessive it could indicate valve-guide trouble.

Even if a low oil pressure reading is indicated it still may not follow that the bottom-end of the engine is worn-out. A big drop or even a complete loss of pressure can be caused by debris in the oil-pressure relief valve, the culprit on early cars sometimes being one of the split-pins which secure the locking-nuts of the connecting-rod to the bearing caps; later, the pins were replaced by self-locking nuts.

Similarly, the 5.3-litre V12 engine has been found to be just as long-lived, and with few inherent design faults. However, beware of an engine that is known to lose water, because this could be head-gasket trouble; if the fault has not been rectified promptly the heads can weld themselves to the block and be extremely difficult to remove. A specialist may have to spend as much as 10 hours on this job alone.

Listen carefully for rattles at the front-end of the engine, which may indicate a worn jack-shaft assembly, and try shaking the water-pump pulley to see if there is play in the bearings. Also, with your ear as close to the sump as possible, listen for suspect bearing trouble; this is very hard to detect and the oil-pressure reading (which should be at least 60 psi at 3,500rpm) is no guide as the gauge can indicate this pressure even if one bearing has run completely.

On taking a Series 3 car for a run, watch for a partial misfire or 'hunt' at about 3,500-4,500rpm on partial load; this could mean that the valves have collected a white, carbon-like deposit which means that eventually they will have to be replaced. This symptom is not to be confused with the very pronounced misfire caused by early problems with the OPUS ignition system's amplifier unit or coil. The valve-guides are long-lasting and should not cause oil to be burnt, so a lot of blue smoke after a steady run in top might indicate bore wear.

It is also worth keeping an eye open for oil leaks. These are usually more of an annoyance than anything else, but can be expensive to rectify; in particular, watch for drips from the bellhousing area, which indicates a leak from the rear of the crankshaft. To replace the seal means removing the engine which, with labour and parts, may well amount to £400 or more.

But despite its apparent complexity, and the overawing nature of the maze of tubes in which the engine appears to be enshrined when you open the bonnet, Jaguar's V12 is in essence a very well-engineered, low-stressed power unit capable of six-figure mileages without major attention. In fact, most serious failures can be traced back not to wear but to an owner allowing the engine to run out of either oil or water.

Driving the car will tell you much about the condition of an E-type's suspension, brakes and steering. For its size, it should feel light on its feet, responsive, and without low-speed understeer. There should be no rear-end steering effects or bottoming, nor any clunks from the rear suspension when moving the foot on and off the accelerator, or when starting from rest. Such noises could indicate worn splines (particularly if accompanied by a regular high-pitched squeak), half-shaft universal joints, or stub-axle bottom pivot bearings. The ball-joints at the front often suffer from neglect, so check them for play by jacking-up each wheel and watching for 'drop' as the wheel is allowed to come down

Towards the rear of the car, common rusting points are all round the wheelarch and under the bumper, where inner and outer skins meet.

Steer well clear of repairs like this! A crudely welded patch will do nothing to secure a badly rusted mounting-point for the rear suspension's trailing-arm.

again — or use a wooden plank as a lever and carefully try raising the wheel while it is suspended freely on stands.

The steering should be light, and there should be little lost movement at the wheel; watch the rack mountings because they can loosen. As for brakes, on 3.8 cars it really depends on the condition of the servo if all else appears well, but expect to have to use a strong right foot to stop the thing. On later vacuum-servo cars the brakes should cope with all normal use provided the wheel cylinders and discs are in good condition — see that the discs are free from patches of rust, which will indicate that a wheel cylinder is not gripping the disc satisfactorily.

Finally, a word about gearboxes. While a few years ago you would have had difficulty in getting a fiver for a good non-synchromesh Jaguar gearbox, the position now is that first and reverse gears have become unobtainable, which means that to recondition a 3.8 E-type box could cost several hundred pounds for special machining. So fight shy of a car that has very noisy first or reverse gears, which indicates chipped, missing or worn teeth.

The spares position for the all-synchromesh box fitted from 1964 (some late 3.8s had them, too) is much better, so the matter is not so critical. But bear in mind that gearbox replacement means taking the engine out, although the cowboy way of doing it was to cut the metal transmission tunnel about and lever the box up through the cockpit — definitely not recommended. This box should be reasonably light in operation, with little noise from the gears, and its synchromesh should enable you to put the lever into first gear at around 30mph without double-declutching.

CHAPTER 8

Spares and maintenance

Sources, manuals and clubs

An E-type which is in good condition is a reliable and mechanically long-lived machine, provided that oil, grease and water are applied to the right points at regular intervals, and a minimum of preventive maintenance is carried out on ancillary equipment such as the ignition system, generator and other electrical parts. Unfortunately, especially in the earlier, pre-V12 years, the E-type inevitably attracted the carefree, getaway type who maybe did not understand too much about the moving parts, and having picked up the expected quota of 'birds', would discard the car, unmaintained, to the next in line, who probably couldn't really afford it, and who thus skimped on servicing once more, and so on.

Fortunately there is virtually no mechanical spare which cannot be found, if not from the factory, from private specialists in E-type parts. The few exceptions include some gearbox components for 3.8 cars, as mentioned, and items relating to the old bellows servo (which to replace with the later type requires the use of a new pedal-box, such as is offered by Phoenix Engineering of Goole).

However, owners of Series 1 cars may face increasing difficulty in finding replacements for their shiny accessories, such as bumpers, lights, door handles and so on. Such parts usually come to light after a search, but don't expect to get them off the shelf from a Jaguar distributor. Interior fittings, including seats, for 3.8 E-types are hard to locate now, even secondhand, so it is not always wise to buy that cheap old shell which seems such a bargain — it may take you months or even years to find all the brightware and accessories to hang on it. Owners of Series 2 and 3 cars will have rather fewer problems in this respect.

A reasonable number of mechanical parts are interchangeable with Jaguar saloons, but often it isn't as easy as it looks and requires much research with parts books and practical experience to determine which you can use. Likewise, a complete monocoque restoration (and in the final analysis this is what most pre-V12 E-types are beginning to require) is best left to the experts, unless you are a skilled welder and panel-beater and are expert at lead-loading (which is how Jaguar contoured the panel joins on the monocoque).

This degree of skill is required because of the nature of the E-type's body design, with its many stress-bearing component panels. Remove too many rusted panels and the whole shell can distort if not properly supported, and if the carefree welder doesn't notice he will end up with a repaired shell which is an immediate write-off. Also, even if new factory panels are obtained and fitted, they will not just drop into place — production tolerances ensure that each will have to be carefully shaped and adapted by hand to achieve the correct fit. Even fitting and lining-up a new bonnet on the car can take a skilled man two days if it happens to be an awkward one.

Engine and suspension overhauls, however, can be tackled by the competent home mechanic, provided due care is taken and you work from an official workshop manual. The rear suspension, complex though it may appear, should not be beyond the scope of the person used to rebuilding a simple engine, although parts for a complete overhaul will inevitably cost several hundred pounds, excluding the differential.

I mentioned workshop manuals — for Series 3 cars, at least, you should be able to order manuals and parts books from a Jaguar

Maintenance of the original bellows servo on 3.8 cars can be difficult, so those not too concerned with originality may want to fit a conventional servo with the necessary new pedal-box as offered by Phoenix Engineering.

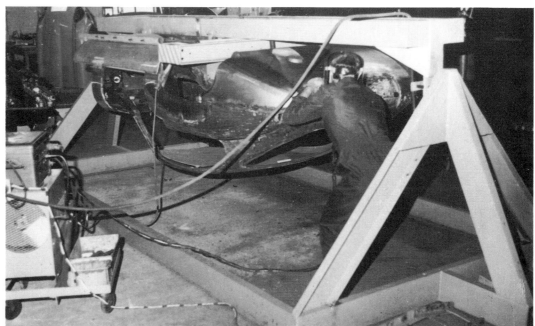

There are exceptions to every rule, but usually a very badly corroded bodyshell (and there are a lot of them) will require full reconditioning by an expert with facilities like these.

Tackling E-type bodywork rarely stops at a new outer sill — on this car, at least 4 inches of the inner sill and a complete new floor have also been fitted.

together for this purpose.

It is difficult to be specific in a book of this nature about the availability or otherwise of any particular item, because the situation changes almost monthly, but so far as Series 2 or earlier cars are concerned it is unlikely that BL will — or indeed can be expected to — go back into production with parts as factory stocks are exhausted. Mechanical items, with some exceptions already discussed, should not be a problem for the foreseeable future because they are often shared with other Jaguar models, but for many body panels, brightware and trim the owner increasingly will have to turn to the various specialists in Jaguar parts. These people maintain their stocks by buying job-lots from dealers who are clearing out or changing their franchise, or by investing considerable sums of money having otherwise unobtainable items specially remanufactured. Some also offer used parts, which is often the only way out where an unobtainable part is too complex to be made in small numbers.

A few sources which can generally be relied upon to carry good stocks of E-type parts are as follows, though do not expect them to be able to duplicate a full factory service:

distributor. For owners of six-cylinder E-types there is *The Complete Official Jaguar E,* published in the USA by Robert Bentley Inc., of Cambridge, Massachusetts, and available in the UK through Connoisseur Carbooks, 32 Devonshire Road, Chiswick, London W4 2HD (Tel: 01-994 6783). Based on original factory material it comprises the driver's handbook, workshop manual and special tuning manual all in one large volume.

At least one firm — FB Components — is reprinting parts manuals, and this company also operates a good overseas mail-order service for E-type and other Jaguar parts. They have a particularly good stock of most rubber door seals. Jaguar themselves have a diminishing stock of pre-Series 3 parts, but it is often worth placing an order through a Jaguar distributor to see what turns up, especially if you can find a parts-counter man willing to go through the bother of checking part numbers, which have been updated several times and are now on microfilm or computer. There is no longer a separate Jaguar spares organization as BL have brought Jaguar, Rover and Triumph

Phoenix Engineering (E-type specialists),
Creykes Cottage,
Rawcliffe Bridge,
Goole, Yorkshire.
(Tel: Goole 83339)

British Sports Car Centre Ltd.,
308 King Street,
Hammersmith,
London W6.
(Tel: 01-741 3997)

G.H. Nolan Ltd.,
1 St George's Way,
London SE15.
(Tel: 01-701 2785)

Oldham & Crowther,
27 Ivatt Way,
Westwood Industrial Estate,
Peterborough, PE3 7PH.
(Tel: Peterborough 262577).

FB Components,
35-41 Edgeway Road,
Marston,
Oxford.
(Tel: Oxford 724646)

Assistance can also be given to the serious E-type owner in Great Britain by the E-type Register, which is a division of the highly successful Jaguar Driver's Club. Technical advice is available, and members have access to further parts sources. They also receive the JDC's professionally produced monthly magazine *Jaguar Driver,* which contains a lot of good E-type reading, plus small-ads listing parts for sale.

Both the JDC and its various Registers (which also cater individually for other Jaguars such as XK, Mk 1/2 saloon, S-type, XJ, etc) hold a variety of functions, including an International E-type Day, which sees many hundreds of E-types converging. The top concours entrants at this event provide an excellent opportunity for the would-be E-type restorer to see for himself what is original and what was painted which colour, and to get first-hand advice from those who have been through it all before.

E-type Register membership details can be obtained from JDC headquarters at the Norfolk Hotel, Harrington Road, London SW1 (Tel: 01-584 9494). North American owners can join one of the 40-plus Jaguar clubs affiliated to the factory-backed Jaguar Clubs of North America Inc., situated at 600 Willow Tree Road, Leonia, New Jersey 07605, USA, or the independent EJAG Club at 1 Acton Road, Westford, Massachusetts 01886, USA. The addresses of other overseas Jaguar clubs can be obtained from Molly Wheeler at JDC headquarters in London.

Running an E-type Jaguar is not a particularly cheap way of motoring — speed always costs money — but it is far easier on the wallet than any other car offering a similar or even a somewhat lesser performance. From every angle, therefore, the E-type Jaguar is a truly remarkable motor car.

This is a detail of the E-type's door pillar, with the rear wing removed to disclose one of the complex box-sections which make up the car.

Glass-fibre bonnets like this one are readily available, and are a good short-term solution to the problem of a rotted bonnet. However, the fitting of an original factory steel bonnet is the only proper answer, as otherwise the value of the car will be seriously affected.

Generally, one can still find most of the E-type's mechanical components, although some items, like this Lucas immersed-type petrol pump used on 3.8 cars, are now virtually unobtainable.

The E-type roadster does not have a complete inner rear wing, the outer wing being single-thickness at the top of the wheelarch. Repairs are effected either by replacing the whole rear-wing panel, or cutting out the corroded area and letting-in a new section, as is being done here; this applied to all body styles.

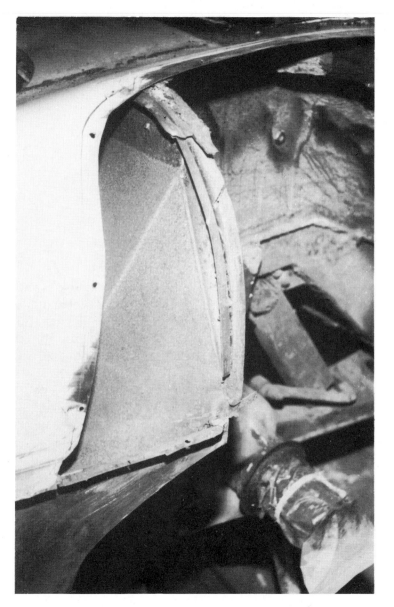

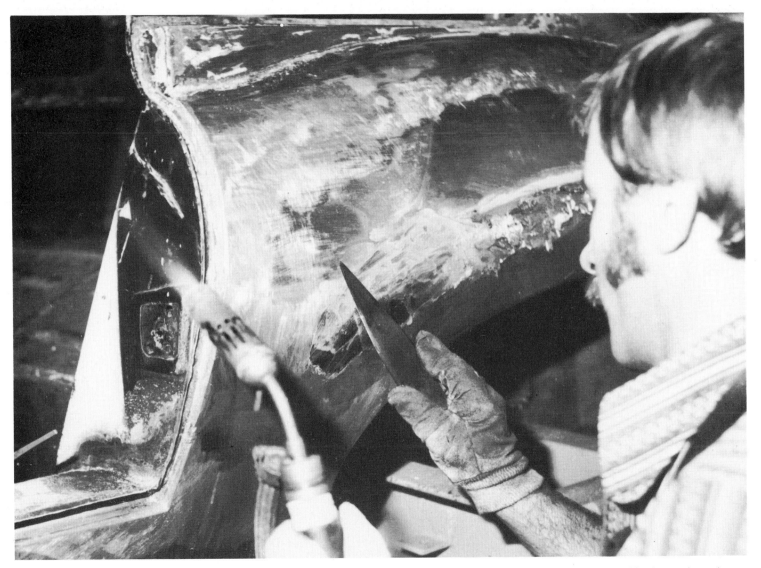

After the repairs illustrated on the previous page the welded join will be finished and then covered by a coating of lead, which was used by Jaguar themselves to contour joins in panels.

The rebuilding of the E-type's fairly complex rear suspension is not overly difficult and can be attempted by any keen home mechanic. This is one such rebuild coming together, the job being made much simpler thanks to the fact that the whole unit drops away from the car in one piece, contained within its steel subframe.

Many early E-types which may look superficially sound can end up looking like this on being stripped down; here, rusted panels and plastic filler are being removed from the rear-end of a 3.8 E-type to leave very little of the original car! This sort of repair is usually best left to the professional.

Cylinder-head overhauls can be accomplished leaving the bottom half of the engine 'in situ'. This is an early 3.8 fixed-head with its head removed for reconditioning; the bonnet is also off, which makes for much better accessibility. Note the early alloy radiator — not many of these are left now.

Jaguar's last sports cars?

APPENDIX A

Technical specifications

3.8 Fixed-head coupe — produced 1961 to 1964
Engine: 6-cyl, 87x106mm, 3,781cc, CR 9:1 (8:1 optional), 3 2in SU carbs, rated 265bhp (gross) at 5,500rpm. Maximum torque 260 lb ft at 4,000rpm.
Transmission: Axle ratio 3.31:1 (alternatives 2.93, 3.27, 3.07, 3.54, 3.77, 4.09).
Overall gear ratios: 3.31, 4.25, 6.16, 11.18, reverse 11.18.
Mph/1,000rpm in top gear: 23.0 (3.31), 21.5 (3.54), 24.8 (3.07), 26.0 (2.93), all RS5 tyres.
Suspension and brakes: Ifs, torsion bars, wishbones and telescopic dampers, anti-roll bar; Irs, coil springs, lower wishbone/drive shaft, radius arms, telescopic dampers, anti-roll bar. Rack-and-pinion steering. 11in disc brakes front and 10-in rear. 6.40-15in tyres on 5in rim wire wheels; 5½in-rim rear wheels optional.
Dimensions: Wheelbase 8ft; front track 4ft 2in; rear track 4ft 2in. Length 14ft 7½in; width 5ft 5¼in; height 4ft.
Unladen weight 24¼cwt.
Basic price: £1,550.

3.8 Open two-seater — produced 1961 to 1964
Specification as for fixed-head coupe 3.8 except for:
Height (hood up) 3ft 11in.
Unladen weight 24cwt.
Basic price: £1,480.

4.2 Fixed-head coupe (Series 1) — produced 1964 to 1967
Specification as for 3.8 except for:
Engine: 6cyl, 92.07x106mm, 4,235cc, CR 9:1 (8:1 optional), 3 2in SU carbs, rated 265bhp (gross) at 5,400rpm. Maximum torque 283 lb ft at 4,000rpm.
Transmission: Axle ratio 3.07:1 (alternatives as for 3.8).
Overall gear ratios 3.07, 3.90, 5.34, 8.23, reverse 9.45.
Unladen weight 25cwt.
Basic price: £1,648.

4.2 Open two-seater (Series 1) — produced 1964 to 1967
Specification as for fixed-head coupe except for:
Height (hood up) 3ft 11in.
Unladen weight 24½cwt.
Basic price: £1,568.

4.2 Two-plus-two (Series 1) — produced 1966 to 1967
Specification as for fixed-head coupe except for:
Dimensions: Wheelbase 8ft 9in; front track 4ft 2¼in; rear track 4ft 2¼in. Length 15ft 4½in; width 5ft 6in; height 4ft 2½in.
Unladen weight 27¾cwt.
Transmission (manual): Axle ratio 3.07:1 (alternatives as for fixed-head coupe).
Overall gear ratios 3.07, 4.07, 6.06, 9.33, reverse 10.71.
Mph/1,000rpm 24.8 (Dunlop SP41 radial-ply tyres).
Automatic ratios 6.91, 4.20, 2.88.
Unladen weight 27½cwt.
Basic price: £1,857 (manual).

4.2 Fixed-head coupe (Series 2) — produced 1968 to 1971
Specification as for Series 1 except for:
Unladen weight 25½cwt. Width 5ft 6¼in.
Emission engine: 171bhp (DIN) at 4,500rpm. Maximum torque 230lb ft at 2,500rpm.
Basic price: £1,740.

4.2 Open two-seater (Series 2) — produced 1968 to 1971
Specification as for Series 1 except for:
Unladen weight 25cwt. Width 5ft 6¼in. Mechanical specification as for Series 2 fixed-head coupe.
Basic price: £1,655.

4.2 Two-plus-two (Series 2) — produced 1968 to 1971

Specification as for Series 1 except for:
Unladen weight: 28¼ cwt. Width 5ft 6¼ in. Mechanical specification as for Series 2 fixed-head coupe.
Basic price: £1,922 (manual).

5.3 Two-plus-two (Series 3) — produced 1971 to 1973

Engine: 12-cyl, 90x70mm, 5,343cc, CR 9:1, 4 Zenith-Stromberg 175CDSE carbs, rated 272bhp (DIN) at 5,850rpm. Maximum torque 304 lb ft (DIN) at 3,600rpm.
Transmission: Axle ratio 3. 07:1 (alternative ratios as for 4.2 but normally 3.31 or 3.54).
Overall gear ratios 3.07, 4.27, 5.86, 9.00, reverse 10.37.
Mph/1,000rpm in top gear: 24.7.
Suspension and brakes: Ifs, torsion bars, anti-dive wishbones and telescopic dampers, anti-roll bar; Irs, coil springs, lower wishbone/drive shaft, radius arms, telescopic dampers, anti-roll bar. Rack-and-pinion steering. 11.2in vented discs front, 10.4in solid discs rear. E70VR-15in tyres on 6in-rim wheels (steel or wire).
Dimensions: Wheelbase 8ft 9in; front track 4ft 6½in; rear track 4ft 5in; width 5ft 6¼in; height 4ft 3in.
Unladen weight 29½ cwt.
Basic price: £2,708.

5.3 Open two-seater (Series 3) — produced 1971 to 1975

Specification as for 2-Plus-2 except for:
Height 4ft 1in.
Unladen weight 28¾ cwt.
Basic price: £2,510.

APPENDIX B

Chassis number sequences — by model and date

Model	Years built	Engine No. prefix	Chassis No. sequence	
			Rhd	Lhd
3.8 OTS	Mar 61-Oct 64	R or RA	850	875
3.8 FHC	Mar 61-Oct 64	R or RA	860	885
4.2 S1 OTS	Oct 64-Dec 67	7E	1E1001	1E10001
4.2 S1 FHC	Oct 64-Dec 67	7E	1E2001	1E30001
4.2 S1 2P2	Oct 64-Dec 67	7E	1E50001	1E75001
'S1½' OTS	Dec 67-Oct 68	7E	1E1864	1E15889
'S1½' FHC	Dec 67-Oct 68	7E	1E21584	1E34250
'S1½' 2P2	Dec 67-Oct 68	7E	1E50975	1E77645
4.2 S2 OTS	Oct 68-Sept 70	7R	1R1001	1R7001
4.2 S2 FHC	Oct 68-Sept 70	7R	1R20001	1R25001

Model	Years built	Engine No. prefix	Chassis No. sequence	
			Rhd	Lhd
4.2 S2 2P2	Oct 68-Sept 70	7R	1R35001	1R40001
5.3 S3 OTS	Mar 71-Feb 75	7S	1S1001	1S20001
5.3 S3 2P2	Mar 71-Sept 73	7S	1S50001	1S70001

Abbreviations:
FHC — Fixed Head Coupe
OTS — Open Two Seater
2P2 — Two-Plus-Two
RHD — Right-Hand-Drive
LHD — Left-Hand-Drive

Engineering changes — by model, date and number

The following data relates significant engineering changes which occurred during the E-type's life. The dates given for the introduction of these changes are only approximate; also, certain cars before the chassis or engine numbers given may have been fitted with the component in question. This is particularly common just before the introduction of a new model.

Abbreviations:
FHC — Fixed Head Coupe
OTS — Open Two Seater
2P2 — Two-Plus-Two
Rhd — Right-Hand-Drive
Lhd — Left-Hand-Drive

3.8 E-type

CHASSIS	Date	Chassis No.	
		Rhd	Lhd
Water deflector fitted on front stub-axle carrier	Aug 1961 (FHC)	860001	885001
	(OTS)	850048	875133
Self-adjusting handbrake introduced	Oct 1961	860004 850090	885015 875332
Larger rear outer hub-bearings	Oct 1961	860005 850092	885021 875386
Larger universal-joint on prop-shaft	Oct 1961	860006 850104	885026 875496
Longer rear road springs	Oct 1961	860008 850137	885039 875542
Brass bush in brake and clutch pedal housing	Dec 1961	860021	885105
Brass bush in brake and clutch pedal housing replaced by impregnated plastic — lubrication no longer required	Dec 1961	860021 850233	885105 875859

Modified brake master-cylinders to incorporate positive location of spring support to piston	Jan 1962	860027 850255	885156 876015
Change of brake-pad material to Mintex M33	Jan 1962	—	—
Brake power lever and pedals altered to increase mechanical advantage Accelerator pedal on Rhd cars altered to facilitate 'heel and toe' operation	May 1962	860375 850475	885871 876999
'Sealed for life' universal-joints on prop-shaft	May 1962	860387 850480	885888 877045
New oil-seal container and felt oil-seal fitted to outer fulcrum shaft	June 1962	860451 850504	885985 877183
Modified clutch master-cylinder to incorporate positive location of rear spring support to piston	July 1962	860647 858548	886219 877489
One-piece forged lower steering column to replace tubular-shaft assembly	July 1962	860647 850548	886214 877488
Solid forged rear-axle half-shafts to replace tubular shafts	July 1962	860658 850555	886247 877550
Handbrake cable, compensator and calipers modified	July 1962	860664	886263
Revised fixing for rear-brake calipers	Sept 1962	860741 850578	886456 877736
Change of rear axle-ratio — USA and Canada now 3.31:1, home market and other countries now 3.07:1. Option of 2.93:1 deleted	Oct 1962	—	—
'Sealed for life' rear-axle half-shaft joints	Nov 1962	—	—

		Rhd	Lhd
Water thrower fitted to rear hubs	Sept 1962	860833 850584	886686 877964
Thicker (½-inch) rear brake discs with new calipers and modified caliper mountings and final-drive casing. Incorporated by axle ratio	June 1963 3.54:1		888673 879441
	3.31:1		888695 879461
	3.07:1	861185 850722	888706 879494
Handbrake compensator inner lever link replaced by inner fork-end and outer fork-end giving greater range of adjustment	Aug 1963	861203 850728	888760 879551
Change of rear-axle ratio: USA and Canada 3.54:1	Sept 1963 (plus (plus	888952 to 880026 879751 to	889124 888994) 879808)
Italy, France, Belgium, Germany and Holland 3.07:1			888967 879759
Home market and countries not included above 3.31:1		861226 850737	889003 879821
New rear-axle breather unit — valve replaced by extension assembly	Nov 1963	861364 850785	889452 880562
Half-shaft universal-joint shrouds	Jan 1964	861424 850806	889698 880755
Brake-fluid reservoir cap fitted with cover	Jan 1964	861427 850657	889697 880760

ENGINE AND GEARBOX

		Engine or Chassis No.	
		Rhd	Lhd
Larger oil pump	June 1961	R.1009	
Cast-iron crankshaft pulley instead of alloy	Oct 1961	R.1459	
Automatic fan-belt tensioner	Oct 1961	R.1845	
C42 dynamo and RB340 regulator fitted. New petrol-pump assembly and tank with modified tank filter and one-piece drain plug	Oct 1961	860005 850092	885021 875386

New crankshaft rear oil seal (asbestos rope)	Dec 1961	R.2564	
Revised throttle arrangement with two slave-shafts instead of three, and flexible coupling etc. deleted. Air balance-pipe redesigned with two bosses instead of three	Jan 1962	R.2934	
Reduced big-end clearances	Feb 1962	R.3162	
Modified cylinder-head gasket with enlarged head stud holes	Mar 1962	R.3691	
Drilled inlet camshaft to reduce cold-starting noise	May 1962	R.5001	
Duplex water-pump belt with modified pulleys	June 1962	R.5250	
Modified sump-filter basket incorporating four semi-circular cutouts	June 1962	R.5400	
Revised clutch-fluid reservoir and brackets	July 1962	860678 850556	886283 877557
Internal fuel-pipe material changed from Vulkollan to Nylon	Sept 1962	860584 850527	886095 877355
Longer inlet-valve guides	Sept 1962	R.6724	
Modified piston rings and connecting-rod with additional big-end lug drillings	Sept 1962	R.7104	
Larger main-bearing cap dowels	Oct 1962	R.7195	
Quick-lift thermostat	Nov 1962	R.8300	
Modified mounting at rear of gearbox	Jan 1963	861062 850647	888082 878889
Radiator header-tank revised with higher-pressure (9 lbs) radiator cap	March 1973	861091 850657	888241 879044
Straight instead of convoluted header tank hose	engine-to-		
Delrin needle-valve fitted to carburettors with new float-chamber lid and hinged lever	June 1963	RA.2464	
New-type (22 D6 instead DMBZ6) distributor	June 1963	—	

Modified oil pump and ¾-inch instead 11/16-inch oil suction pipe	June 1963	RA.2078
Exhaust valves of improved material	Sept 1963	RA.2972
Modified piston with chamfer and oil drain holes below control ring to improve oil consumption	March 1964	RA.5649
Laycock diaphragm clutch introduced (modified flywheel to suit both Borg & Beck and Laycock clutches)	March 1964	RA.5801
Intermediate lower timing chain damper secured to bosses in block instead of to timing-chain bracket	May 1964	RA.6025
Modified distributor (Lucas No. 40888A) fitted to 9:1 engines	June 1964	RA.6834

BODY AND FITTINGS

		Chassis No. Rhd	Lhd
Internal bonnet locks	Sept 1961	FHC 860005	885021
		OTS 850092	875386
Seat-belt attachments points provided	Jan 1962	860113 850301	885318 875359
Revised method of attaching bonnet-hinges to front subframe with bolt retaining hinges to cross-tube	Feb 1962	860139 850239	885385 876458
Heel wells fitted. Body Nos: 1635 1647 2879 2889	Feb 1962	860176 850358	885504 876582
Combined ignition switch and steering lock fitted to all cars exported to Germany.	March 1962		885567 876665
Electrically heated backlight optional	April 1962	—	—
Detachable hardtop available	May 1962	—	—
Minor body changes, FHC only, to outer rear wings, bootlid gutter, bootlid shell, hinge for bootlid, tail panel, lid for petrol filler, door shell, door light, etc.	May 1962	860476	886014

Alteration to OTS door (requiring revised chrome outer finisher)	May 1962	850507	877202
New rear bulkhead-section to allow extra rearward travel for seats; temporary modification had been incorporated in driver's side only shortly after car's introduction	June 1962	860581 850527	886093 877356
Revised jack of cantilever type	June 1962	860661 850549	886247 877519
Pattern change on embossed aluminium finishers on instrument panel, front finisher panel, gearbox cover	Oct 1962	860913 850610	887132 878302
Revised bootlid prop on FHC	Dec 1962	861014	887317
Improved quarter-light catches to prevent closing at speed on FHC	Oct 1963		
Modification to allow opening of OTS boot if cable fails (via hole in numberplate panel using 3/16-inch diameter right-angle rod)	Jan 1964	850768	880291

NOTES — 3.8 E-TYPE

i When the optional close-ratio gearbox is fitted, a different clutch-housing, primary shaft and oil-seal are used.

ii Dunlop SP radial tyres were offered as optional equipment from May 1963.

iii Manufacture of the Lucas immersed centrifugal impeller fuel pump ceased during the early-seventies, and the factory issued a kit to convert the fuel system to the external SU reciprocating-diaphragm pump (type AUF 301) similar to that used on 4.2 cars. Position for the SU pump was in the right-hand corner of the spare-wheel well, adjacent to the rear-wheel arch.

iv Wing mirrors (Part No. C.19909) were available as optional extras from 1961 (front-wing mounting).

v In 1962 a booklet was issued by the works entitled *Tuning and Preparation of E-type Cars for Competition Use* (now out of print). It listed various minor body and mechanical alterations and a number of special parts available from the factory.

4.2 Series 1 E-type

CHASSIS

	Date	Chassis No. Rhd	Lhd
Front disc-brake shields fitted	Feb 1965 FHC	1E.20100	1E.30302
Change of axle ratio from 3.31:1 to 3.07:1 (except USA and Canada, (3.54:1)	April 1965 FHC	1E.20329	1E.30772
	OTS	1E.1152	1E.1073
7-tooth pinion introduced to improve steering when radial-ply tyres fitted	March 1966	1E.20993 1E.1413	1E.31765 1E.11535
New road wheel introduced with forged centre hub and straight spokes	May 1967 2P2	1E.21518 1E.1814 1E.50912	1E.34339 1E.11535 1E.77475
Powr-Lok diff. discontinued as standard except USA 3.54	Sept 1967	1E.21620 1E.1887	1E.34603 1E.15982
Grease nipples reintroduced on half-shaft universal joints	Jan 1968	1E.21669 1E.1926 1E.51067	1E.34851 1E.16721 1E.77705

ENGINE AND GEARBOX

	Date	Engine or Chassis No. Rhd	Lhd
Chamfered idler gear to reduce possible gearbox noise	Nov 1964		
Modified roller-bearing fitted to gearbox constant-pinion shaft	March 1965	EJ.945	
Constant-pinion shaft changed to include oil thrower	Feb 1966	EJ.3170	
New brake and clutch master-cylinders and pedal housings fitted to standardise with 2-plus-2	March 1966	1E.21000 1E.1413	1E.32010 1E.11741
Shield fitted to alternator	May 1966	7E.6333	
Modified carburettor assembly with low-lift cam to reduce engine speed when choke operated	Sept 1966 2P2	7E.7298 7E.50022	
Retaining washer fitted to additionally secure gear-lever	Nov 1966	EJ.7920	
Modified clutch and brake master-cylinders with shorter pushrods to revise pedal angles, also improve accelerator-pedal angle	Nov 1966	1E.21342 1E.1561	1E.32942 1E.13011
Valve-guides fitted with circlips to ensure positive location in cylinder-head	Jan 1967	7E.7450 7E.50022	
Oil seals fitted to inlet-valve guides	March 1967	7E.11668 7E.52687	
US Federal spec. introduced	Jan 1968		1E.34583 1E.15180
Replaceable filter fitted to fuel line	Feb 1968	1E.21662 1E.1905 1E.50143	1E.34772 1E.16057 1E.77701
Vertical-flow radiator, new water-pump assembly, twin cooling-fans with relay, revised breather-pipe and thermostat (already incorporated in LHD cars)	April 1968	1E.31807 1E.2051 1E.51213	
Solid-skirt Hepworth and Grandage pistons fitted instead of Brico split-skirt	June 1968	—	—
Revised water-pump pulley and belt to increase pump speed and flow-rate	June 1968	7E.17158 7E.54837	

BODY AND FITTINGS

	Date	Chassis No. Rhd	Lhd
Revision of finisher-panel assembly on gearbox and prop-shaft tunnel, deletion of chrome bezel at top of panel for gearlever gauntlet and chrome ferrel at top of gauntlet	Nov 1964	1E.10360 1E.1061	
Pocket under rear side windows deleted. Change from mocquette to plastic on rear wheelarches, rear door hinges, etc (FHC)	Jan 1965	1E.20117	1E.30402
Hazard warning light fitted as standard	Dec 1965		1E.32194 1E.12025
Window-frame seals changed from felt to flocked runner (FHC)	Feb 1966	1E.20953	1E.31920

	Date	Chassis No. Rhd	Lhd
Switch incorporated in heated back-light circuit	April 1966	1E.21223	1E.32609
Ambla gear-lever gauntlet		1E.21442 1E.1686 1E.50586	1E.33549 1E.13589 1E.76911
Deletion of headlight covers	July 1967	1E.21584 1E.1864 1E.50975	1E.34250 1E.15889 1E.77645
Revised dash assembly incl. heater box and controls, cubby box lid, choke, switches	April 1968	1E.21784 1E.2039	
US Federal spec. doors, casings and linings fitted to RHD cars	June 1968		
Water-temperature gauge with zonal markings only replacing calibrated gauge	July 1968	—	1E.34945 1E.16538 1E.77838

NOTES — 4.2 SERIES 1 E-TYPE

i   Oil-cooler and installation kit for 3.8 and 4.2 cars (not Series 2) available as an extra from April 1969.

ii   From late-1967/early-1968 various updating features were incorporated into the 4.2 E-type's specification; although colloquially known as the 'Series 1½', these changes did not denote a new model as such, and it is not possible to define a distinct '1½' specification because of progressive modifications carried out before the appearance of the true Series 2 car.

iii   Close-ratio gearbox discontinued commencing box no. EE 1001.

iv   Cars with air-conditioning have sealant cooling system, with expansion tank having 13-lb cap mounted on bulkhead (header tank still retained) June 1967.

4.2 Series 2 E-type

CHASSIS	Date	Chassis No. Rhd	Lhd
Non-eared hub-caps standardized on RHD cars	Jan 1969 FHC OTS 2P2	1R.20073 1R.1054 1R.1054 1R.35099	
Revised handbrake-lever assembly introduced with increased length and end portion angled upwards (2-plus-2)	May 1970	1R.35816	1R.43924
Larger-diameter torsion-bars	Aug 1970	1R.1776	

	Date	Engine or Chassis No. Rhd	Lhd
fitted to RHD cars (0.744-inch to 0.780-inch)		1R.20955	

ENGINE AND GEARBOX	Date	Engine or Chassis No. Rhd	Lhd
Lucas 11AC alternator with side-entry cables	Jan 1969	1R.20007 1R.1013 1R.35011	1R.25284 1R.7443 1R.40208
Improved clutch with higher-rated diaphragm spring to reduce tendency to slip	Mar 1969 2P2	7R.2588 7R.35731	
'Load-shedding' ignition/starter switch introduced (isolates most auxiliaries while starter engaged)	April 1969	1R.26533 1R.9860 1R.42382	
Camshaft covers secured by countersunk screw at front centre position	May 1969	7R.4159 7R.36600	
Cylinder-block drain tap replaced by plug	June 1969	7R.5542 7R.37655	
Engine No. stamping relocated on crankcase bellhousing flange on LH side of engine, adjacent dip-stick	Aug 1969	7R.6306 7R.38106	
New camshafts with redesigned profiles to give quieter valve operation over wider range of valve clearances and longer periods between adjustment	Nov 1969	7R.8688 7R.38855	
Camshaft covers drilled for warm-air duct (fitted on emission engines)	Jan 1970	7R.8768 7R.38895	
Ballast-resistor ignition fitted	Jan 1970	1R.20486 1R.1393 1R.35643	1R.27051 1R.11052 1R.42850
Key alarm facility ignition switch, USA/Canada	Jan 1970		
Revised clutch-operating rod to accommodate wider setting tolerances	Mar 1970	7R.9710 7R.39112	
New crankshaft distance-piece with 'O' ring	Aug 1970	7R.13199 7R.40326	
Revised thermostat (OTS and FHC)	Oct 1970	7R.14049	

		Chassis No.	
Revised exhaust camshaft without oilway drilling in back of cams, to reduce oil consumption (OTS and FHC)	Oct 1970	7R.14075	

BODY AND FITTINGS

		Chassis No. Rhd	Lhd
Steering-column lock fitted	Dec 1968 FHC	1R.20095	
to RHD cars	OTS 2P2	1R.1085 1R.35099	
Gas-filled bonnet stay instead of counter-springs	June 1969	1R.20270 1R.1188 1R.35353	1R.26387 1R.9570 1R.42118
Petrol tank with design modification to upper panel	Mar 1969	1R.20119 1R.1068 1R.35798	1R.25524 1R.7993 1R.406688
Perforated leather trim and modified head restraints	May 1969	1R.20212 1R.1138	1R.26005 1R.8869
Provision for head-restraints in seats	Aug 1969	1R.20366 1R.1302 1R.35458	1R.26684 1R.10152 1R.42560
Mercury-cell clock replaced by battery-operated instrument	Oct 1969	1R.24425 1R.1351 1R.35564	1R.26835 1R.10537 1R.42677
Demister-tube extension fitted to 2-plus-2	Oct 1969	1R.35650	1R.42552
Key-alarm facility ignition switch (USA cars)	May 1970		

NOTES — 4.2 SERIES 2 E-TYPE

i   Close-ratio gearbox available as optional extra (Part No. C.28648).

ii   New model year 70/71 identified on Federal cars by changing prefix on some cars to 2R.

5.3 Series 3 E-type

CHASSIS

		Chassis No. Rhd	Lhd
Modified brake-pedal components to improve left-foot clearance (RHD automatic cars only)	July 1971 2P2 OTS	IS.50176 IS.1005	

Handbrake assembly made common to RHD and LHD cars	Dec 1971	IS.50872 IS.1152	IS.72357 IS.20122
3.07:1 axle offered as alternative to 3.31:1 on manual cars	April 1972		
Revised adjuster-cam with larger cam profile on torsion-bar	June 1972	IS.51263 IS.1348	IS.73372 IS.20569
Modified pinion-valve assembly on rack and pinion due to isolated instances of self-steer	Dec 1972	IS.51318 IS.1443	IS.73721 IS.20921
Revised power rack and pinion assembly ('W' prefix)	Jan 1973		
Axle ratio on all USA/Canada cars now 3.31:1 (3.54:1 no longer fitted to manual cars); 3.07:1 fitted for all other countries	Mar 1973	— IS.21576	IS.74261
Two-outlet exhaust-pipe with modified silencer replacing four-outlet 'fantail' pipe	Mar 1973	IS.51318 IS.1741	IS.74662 IS.22046
Phosphor-bronze rear hub-spacer replacing steel spacer to eliminate 'click' in rear suspension	June 1973	—	—

ENGINE AND GEARBOX

		Engine or Rhd	Chassis No. Lhd
Modified crankshaft thrust-washer	Dec 1971	7S.4510	
Improved piston assembly (lighter)	May 1972	7S.6310	
Revised starter motor and flywheel (driven plate on automatic cars)	May 1972	7S.7001	
Forward section of engine rainshield now secured to an additional support mounted on front inlet manifold	June 1972	IS.51247 IS.1304	IS.73337 IS.20558
Revised shell bearings to connecting-rod big-ends — oil feed-hole deleted	June 1972	7S.7155	
Printed-circuit ballast resistor (Lucas No. 47229) introduced	Aug 1972	7S.7560	
N10Y plugs specified instead of N9Y	Oct 1972	—	—

Modified water-pump and simplified water-hose system	Oct 1972	7S.7785	
Deletion of small-end oil-feed drilling in connecting-rods	Oct 1972	7S.7856	
Revised main bearings with improved lining material	Dec 1972	7S.8189	
Sealed fuel-system with carbon cannister	Dec 1972		IS.21029
New needle-roller bearings in gearbox	Jan 1973	KL.4241	
Thermostatic vacuum switch fitted to RH rear coolant branch-pipe and associated hoses deleted from all non-exhaust-emission engines	Feb 1973	7S.8444	
New air-injection pump with integral air filter fitted to all exhaust-emission engines	Feb 1973	7S.9034	
Coil-and-ballast resistor moved to RH rear of engine for improved accessability to engine drive-belts	Feb 1973	7S.9679	
Revised Borg-Warner Model 12 automatic gearbox fitted, identical to XJ12-type	Feb 1973	7S.9715	
New petrol-filter assembly with metal filter bowl, dispensing with fuel stop tap. Filter relocated to extreme right of luggage-boot bulkhead panel	Mar 1973	IS.51617 IS.1665	IS.74312 IS.21662
Engines to ECE 15 European emissions spec. for Germany only	March 1973		1S.74769 1S.22272
XJ12 crankshaft damper fitted for standardization	May 1973	7S.10799	
Improved oil-pump assembly with new housing	July 1973	7S.12065	
Cars for USA/Canada fitted with revised camshaft with different cam profile	Oct 1973	7S.1400	
Modified synchromesh-operating sleeve to prevent jumping out of forward gears	Oct 1973	7S.14000	KL.6772

New gearbox countershaft of revised material	Oct 1973	7S.14341	KL.7098
High-load coil and amplifier to improve plug performance	Feb 1974	7S.16210	
Engines to ECE 15 European emissions spec. to all markets except USA/Canada/Japan (OTS)	Oct 1974	1S.2450	1S.23419
Revised valve tappets	Nov 1974	7S.17074	

BODY AND FITTINGS

		Chassis No.	
		Rhd	Lhd
Red marking deleted from water-temperature gauge (USA cars)	July 1971	— —	IS.71370 IS.20025
Connector inserted in windscreen-washer tubing to facilitate removal of bonnet	Nov 1971 2P2 OTS	IS.50203 IS.1005	IS.71476 IS.20025
Demister flap controlled by short cable and connecting-rod instead cable and pinion gears	Mar 1972	IS.50875 IS.1163	IS.72450 IS.20135
Improved symmetrical heater and choke controls	Mar 1972	IS.50379 IS.1040	IS.72319 IS.20091
Securing brackets fitted to centre cross-beam and lower rear-damper mounting for shipping (not towing)	April 1972	IS.50968 IS.1210	IS.72662 IS.20169
Fresh-air vents fitted, with control levers in cockpit	April 1972	IS.51016 IS.1236	IS.72682 IS.20173
Waso steering-column lock fitted in place of Britax	April 1972	IS.51049 IS.1232	IS.72687 IS.20175
Remote-control door mirror fitted to all USA/Canada cars	April 1972	—	IS.72661 IS.20169
Seat-belt alarm system fited to USA cars, rear seats fixed	May 1972	—	IS.72661 IS.20169
Revised air ducts to rear brakes with increased ground clearance; now fitted during assembly and no longer supplied for dealer to fit	April 1973	IS.51610 IS.1663	IS.74266 IS.21606
Five-mph impact front and rear overriders introduced, USA	1974	—	IS.74586 IS.23240

How fast? How economical? How heavy?

	3.8 OTS	3.8 FHC	S1 4.2 OTS	S1 4.2 FHC	S1 4.2 2+2	S2 4.2 OTS	S2 4.2 FHC	S2 4.2 AUTO
Mean max speed (mph)	149	150	149	150	139	142 (126)*	143	136 (128)*
Acceleration (sec)								
0-30	2.6	2.8	2.9	2.7	2.7	2.8 (2.6)	2.8	4.2 (3.4)
0-40	3.8	4.4	4.0	3.7	3.8	3.9 (4.0)	—	5.7 (5.0)
0-50	5.6	5.6	5.6	4.8	5.7	5.2 (5.4)	5.5	6.8 (6.7)
0-60	7.1	6.9	7.4	7.0	7.4	7.2 (7.2)	7.2	8.9 (8.8)
0-70	8.7	8.5	9.4	8.6	9.8	8.9 (9.6)	—	11.0 (11.2)
0-80	11.1	11.1	12.4	11.0	12.4	11.5 (12.4)	12.2	13.1 (14.5)
0-90	13.9	13.2	15.1	13.9	15.4	14.3 (15.8)	—	15.2 (18.1)
0-100	15.9	16.2	17.1	17.2	19.4	16.9 (19.7)	17.0	19.1 (22.8)
0-110	19.9	19.2	23.1	21.0	24.2	21.5 (25.5)	—	24.4 (30.9)
0-120	24.2	25.9	30.1	25.2	31.5	29.0 (—)	30.0	30.0 (—)
Standing ¼-mile (sec)	15.0	14.7	15.0	14.9	15.4	14.9 (15.5)	14.9	16.4 (16.4)
Axle ratio	3.31	3.31	3.07	3.07	3.07	3.07 (3.54)	3.07	2.88 (3.31)
Direct top gear (sec)								
10-30	5.6	—	—	5.8	6.6	5.8 (6.0)	—	—
20-40	5.6	5.5	—	5.5	6.6	5.6 (5.2)	—	—
30-50	5.4	5.4	5.2	5.4	6.5	5.5 (5.2)	—	—
40-60	5.4	5.5	4.7	5.3	6.1	5.3 (5.2)	—	—
50-70	5.3	5.4	5.7	6.0	6.1	5.9 (5.2)	—	—
60-80	5.0	5.6	6.1	6.6	6.5	6.2 (5.8)	—	—
70-90	5.2	5.8	6.2	6.6	6.9	6.4 (6.4)	—	—
80-100	5.7	6.1	6.8	7.3	7.4	6.5 (7.1)	—	—
90-110	6.6	6.3	7.7	7.3	8.6	7.3 (9.8)	—	—
Overall fuel consumption (mpg)	19.7	17.9	21.8	18.5	18.8	18.5 (17.2)	18.9	18.3
Kerb weight (cwt)	24	24.1	25.4	25.1	27.4	25.6	25.7	27.8

*Figures in brackets, North American specification

	S3 OTS (manual)	S3 2+2 (manual)	S3 AUTO (USA)		S3 OTS (manual)	S3 2+2 (manual)	S3 AUTO (USA)
Mean max speed (mph)	146 (135)*	142	135*	Direct top gear (sec)			
Acceleration (sec)				10-30	6.1	7.3	—
0-30	2.7 (3.3)	2.7	2.9	20-40	6.0	6.2	—
0-40	3.5 (4.5)	3.8	4.3	30-50	5.6	5.9	—
0-50	4.7 (6.0)	4.9	5.6	40-60	5.6	5.8	—
0-60	6.4 (7.4)	6.8	7.1	50-70	5.7	5.8	—
0-70	8.0 (9.2)	8.4	9.2	60-80	6.0	6.2	—
0-80	9.9 (11.5)	10.6	11.2	70-90	6.4	6.5	—
0-90	12.7 (—)	13.7	14.6	80-100	7.4	6.9	—
0-100	15.4 (18.5)	16.4	17.5	90-110	10.4	8.3	—
0-110	19.3 (22.8)	20.3	22.0	Overall fuel consumption (mpg)	14.5	15.2	14.0
0-120	25.8 (—)	26.5	27.9	Kerb weight (cwt)	28.8	29.5	29.5
Standing ¼-mile (sec)	14.2 (15.4)	14.6	15.1				
Axle ratio	3.07 (3.54)	3.07	3.31				

*Figures in brackets, North American specification

(Performance figures courtesy of *Autocar, Autosport, Motor, Road & Track* and Jaguar Cars.)

APPENDIX E

Production figures

Model	RHD	LHD	Total	Model	RHD	LHD	Total
3.8 Open two-seater	942	6885	7827	5.3 S3 Open two-seater	1871	6119	7990
3.8 Fixed-head coupe	1798	5871	7669	5.3 S3 2-plus-2	2115	5182	7297
4.2 Open two-seater	1182	8366	9548				
4.2 Fixed-head coupe	1957	5813	7770	Total 3.8 Cars:	**15,496**		
4.2 2-plus-2	1378	4220	5598	Total 4.2 Cars:	**22,916**		
				Total 4.2 S2 Cars:	**18,808**		
4.2 S2 Open two-seater	775	7852	8627	Total 5.3 S3 Cars:	**15,287**		
4.2 S2 Fixed-head coupe	1070	3785	4855				
4.2 S2 2-plus-2	1040	4286	5326	**Grand Total All Cars:**	**72,507**		